London's
BUS
PURCHASES

24
PIMLICO
11
Fulham Chelsea
Victoria Charing
Fleet Street Bank
HAMMERSMITH
VLT 220

London's BUS PURCHASES 1946–1994

STEWART J. BROWN

fawndoon

FRONT COVER: A 1940s Guy Arab and a 1990s Leyland Olympian illustrate just how much the appearance of London's buses changed in the five decades covered in these pages. *Keith McGillivray*

BACK COVER, ABOVE: London's few lowbridge buses were used on specific routes where bridge clearances precluded the use of conventional highbridge vehicles. AEC Regent III RLH74 is at the Northwick Park Station terminus of the 230, which ran to Rayners Lane Station. The route was operated by RLHs from 1953 to 1969. *Chris Aston/Omnicolour*

BACK COVER, BELOW: Small buses played a big part in London's transport in the late 1980s and early 1990s. The most stylish were the 52 Optare CityPacers, 25 of which were allocated to the C2 Camden Hoppa in 1987. The C2 ran from Regent Street to Parliament Hill Fields, where this photograph was taken. The CityPacers were replaced by Optare StarRiders in 1994. *Tony Wilson*

FRONTISPIECE: In the foreground Routemasters hurrying through Parliament Square and in the background Britain's most famous clock. Nearest the camera in this early 1970s view is RM220, followed by RML2301.

OPPOSITE: In 1976-77 LT took delivery of 164 MCW Metropolitans. They were spectacularly unsuccessful and all had left the fleet by 1983. MD162 in Bridge Street on the approach to Parliament Square shows MCW's trademark asymmetric windscreen, designed to improve the driver's view of the kerb.

London's bus purchases 1946–1994
First published by Fawndoon Books 2019

ISBN 978-0-9934831-4-1

© Stewart J Brown 2019

All rights reserved. Copyright theft is crime. No part of this book may be reproduced or transmitted in any form, including by scanning, photocopying or any other means, nor may any part of it be posted on the internet or on any social media, without the prior approval of the publisher.

Designed by Helen Swansbourne
Reprographics by Peter Rowlands

Printed by Bell & Bain, Glasgow

Also published by Fawndoon Books
Scotland's Buses in the 1960s (2016)
Advancing in a Forward Direction (2017)
Glasgow's Buses (2018)
www.fawndoon.com

7 Introduction	68 Experimental double-deckers	108 Iveco
13 London Transport: a brief overview	70 Daimler/Leyland Fleetline	110 Miscellaneous small buses
24 Wartime classes	74 Leyland National	113 Miscellaneous coaches
29 Non-standard deliveries 1946-53	78 Bristol LH	117 DAF
34 BUT trolleybuses	80 Miscellaneous double-deckers	122 Scania
35 The RT family	84 XRM and other unrealised projects	123 Volvo
49 AEC Regal IV	87 MCW	129 Dennis
52 BEA coaches	94 Leyland Titan and Olympian	138 Leyland Titan PD3A
54 AEC Routemaster	100 Leyland Lynx	139 Demonstrators
62 AEC Reliance	101 Mercedes-Benz	142 Registration blocks 1939-1964
64 AEC Merlin and Swift	105 Renault	159 Vehicle index
		160 Tailpiece

Contents

Metropolitan-Cammell-Weymann used the Tower of London as a backdrop for this 1950 advert in *Bus & Coach* which featured Weymann-bodied RT474 with roof-mounted route number display. "Built on Tradition and abreast of the times" was MCW's claim.

Introduction

London Transport was Britain's biggest bus operator. At its peak in the mid 1950s it was running more than 10,000 vehicles. This book lists every bus and coach bought by London Transport in its various public sector forms from the end of World War 2 to the point where its bus-operating subsidiaries were privatised in the early 1990s. For the sake of tidiness I've included some pre-1946 classes in their entirety, namely the B (Bristol K), D (Daimler CW), G (Guy Arab) and, most importantly, that London classic, the AEC RT-type. The lists are arranged broadly chronologically, starting with the wartime classes and ending in the rear-engined era with models from Dennis, Scania and Volvo. For most types some brief technical details are provided.

To keep this book simple and reasonably compact, the information generally relates to vehicles as delivered. So, with but a few exceptions, there are no mentions of RT/RTL body swaps, vehicle renumbering, or of things like changes to livery or seating capacity during the vehicles' lives. This book is for you if, like me, you have long had a general interest in London's buses in the orderly pre-privatisation era. But it won't help you tell the difference between a 3RT3/1 and a 3RT3/3, interesting as it may be. The most easily accessible sources of that level of detail are the many London Transport class histories published over the years by the PSV Circle or Ian Smith's incredible website, countrybus.org.

London's buses have long had an influence which extended well beyond the capital. In the 1950s LT's redundant wartime Guy Arabs were being bought in large numbers by the Scottish Omnibuses group, which led to ex-London Guys running as far north as Thurso. In 1953 Belfast Corporation bought 100 of London's D-class Daimler CWA6s to speed up the replacement of the city's trams by buses. Later in the 1950s relatively young RTs and RTLs were bought by many independent operators with an eye for a bargain, as well as by the municipal transport departments in Bradford and Dundee. The influence of these stylish buses stretched as far south as the Channel Islands, with Jersey Motor Transport, and as far north as the Buchan area of north-east Scotland, with Simpson's of Rosehearty.

Then came the much-maligned DMS family of Daimler Fleetlines. When they started to be withdrawn after as little as seven years in service they found further use with a number of National Bus Company and Scottish Bus Group subsidiaries, the West Midlands and Greater Manchester PTEs, and countless smaller operators. The most unlikely London vehicle to find further service was the Routemaster, but that's what happened in the late 1980s as old-established operators in various parts of Britain, from Inverness to Southampton, used them to compete against newcomers when local bus services outside London were deregulated in 1986. So it continued. London's Titans, Metrobuses and Nationals all enjoyed second lives outside the capital and – although they are outside the scope of this volume – so, too, have the more recent generations of Dennis Dart SLFs and low-floor double-deckers. (And that's not to mention overseas fleet sales to Ceylon/Sri Lanka, Hong Kong, South Africa, Malta, Spain and Yugoslavia.)

My point? Wherever you live in the UK the chances are that at some time in the past ex-London buses have been operating somewhere nearby. So I'd argue that you don't have to live in London to be interested in London's buses. They have, of course, been the subject of many, many books over the years. Search on ebay for *London bus book* and you'll get around 800 hits; a quick glance at the listings suggests almost 100 different titles which transport enthusiasts would count as relevant to their interests. These range from picture albums to well-researched vehicle class histories from Capital Transport. Over the years there have been fleet lists galore, from Ian Allan ABCs, through to the present-day listings from publishers such as LOTS and British Bus Publishing.

In collating the information I've been struck by the sheer size of an organisation which was buying hundreds of buses every year. In the peak year for new bus deliveries, 1950, LT

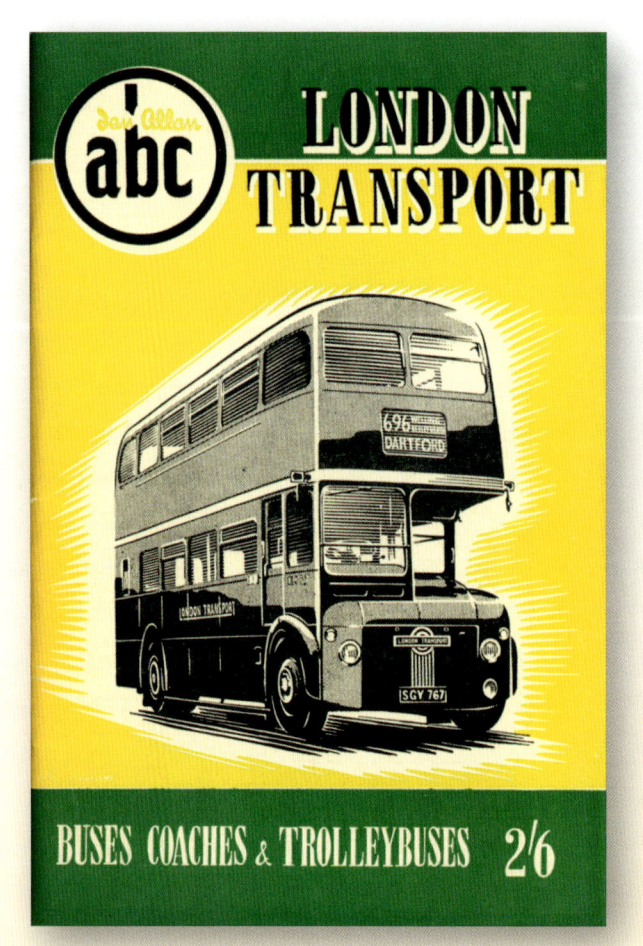

The Ian Allan *ABC of London Transport* covering the undertaking's bus fleet was packed with information, making it much more than just a list of bus numbers. The illustration on the cover of the 1955 edition is a rendition of RM1 with incorrect registration number SGY 767 (the illustrator's car, perhaps?). Its original reduced destination display is showing details for trolleybus route 696, Woolwich to Dartford.

May 17th, 1950   PASSENGER TRANSPORT   851

The Recruit

Every new bus for London Transport has to pass many tests and inspections before it can qualify for a road licence.

The new bus, after the completion of the maker's tests, is driven to our Aldenham Works, where London Transport engineers give it a critical examination. After this it is paraded for the Ministry of Transport Certifying Officer. Each bus is inspected and strictly measured. The readings are checked against the official figures—its length, width, both inside and out, the distance between the seats, its height from the road and so on. When these measurements are agreed the whole bus is weighed—it must not weigh more than 12 tons fully loaded—and it is then given a final road test before being delivered to one of the 80 London Transport garages.

But whenever a new type of bus is introduced, one from the first batch undergoes a still more rigorous examination and is tested under conditions far more severe than it will ever meet when carrying passengers.

Both the Ministry of Transport and London Transport must be sure that the recruit is sound in wind and limb before he goes into service. And it is not until they are completely satisfied that the bus is given its road licence and can begin its working life.

Issued by the London Transport Executive

received just under 2,000 vehicles. As the advert on the previous page from a 1950 issue of *Passenger Transport* shows, each of these new buses had to be inspected by LT's engineers, licensed and insured, and then allocated to a garage. It was then necessary to keep track of it over a life which ranged from seven years or less (some Fleetlines, Metropolitans and Merlins) to 30 years or more (some RTs and Routemasters). And while the size of the fleet has fluctuated over the years, from my northern perspective there have always been more buses running in London than in the whole of Scotland. Buses in London are big business.

This is the fourth title from Fawndoon Books, and the first to venture south of the Scottish border. It is quite different in character from the first three, but benefits from the expertise of the same two friends who have contributed enormously to the quality of the previous Fawndoon titles, designer Helen Swansbourne and reprographics expert Peter Rowlands. Between them they have brought life to what would otherwise have been little more than a list of long-vanished buses. In addition I thank Martin Curtis, Leon Daniels, Chris Drew and Robin Hannay for their help. I was also able to garner information from the archives at the Glasgow Vintage Vehicle Trust and the Scottish Vintage Bus Museum, and the online archive of *Commercial Motor* magazine. Two other important online reference sources are the London Transport Service Vehicles website (ltsv.com) and Ian Smith's countrybus.org. Where known, photographers are acknowledged individually, with a particular mention for Mike Eyre and Tony Wilson who generously made available a wide selection of images. Among those supplied by Mike Eyre are the images credited to Geoffrey Morant, provided by courtesy of Richard Morant. Uncredited photographs were taken by me or have come from my collection. The illustrations on the front cover were prepared specially for this book by Keith McGillivray.

Gavin Booth and Peter Rowlands kindly read a draft of the text and provided helpful comments, while a special thanks goes to Keith Grimes who also read the text and whose suggestions have improved the accuracy of the information. Despite this impressive support there may be the odd error or misinterpretation of events, and these are down to me.

Stewart J Brown
Largs, North Ayrshire 2019

Vehicle body type codes

The codes developed over 60 years ago by the PSV Circle to describe vehicle seating layouts are used in the tables which follow. They show the vehicle seating capacity – split upper/lower deck for double-deckers – and on vehicles designed to carry large numbers of standing passengers this is followed by a plus sign and the maximum number of standees that could be carried. These figures are bracketed by the following letters:

Prefix

B	bus
C	coach
CH	double-deck coach
CO	convertible open-top bus
DP	dual-purpose vehicle
H	highbridge-style double-decker with a centre gangway on both decks
HDC	half-deck coach
L	lowbridge double-decker with an offside sunken gangway on the upper deck
O	open-top bus

Suffix

C	centre entrance
D	dual-door
F	front or forward entrance
L	passenger wheelchair lift
R	rear entrance
RD	rear entrance with platform doors
RO	rear entrance with open staircase
T	toilet compartment

Thus B33+34D indicates a single-deck bus with 33 seats, space for 34 standing passengers, and two doors.

LONDON TRANSPORT MAGAZINE

September 1969 — Threepence

New express bus for London Airport
(REPORT AND PICTURES IN THIS ISSUE)

History has judged London's Merlins harshly which makes it easy to forget that they were, albeit briefly, the exciting modern face of public transport. MBS514 is posed at Heathrow Airport for the launch of the new A1 express service which ran non-stop between the airport and the Tube station at Hounslow West. The A1 operated from August 1969 to December 1977 when the Piccadilly Line was extended to the airport. *London Transport Magazine* was produced monthly for LT's employees who were encouraged to write to its editor with the offer of a payment of half a guinea (55p) for letters which were published.

By the standards of the late 1930s the RT was a strikingly modern vehicle. In September 1946 AEC produced a supplement to its customer magazine, *The AEC Gazette*, which was devoted to its new postwar Regent III. The full-colour cover illustration was based on a photograph of a prewar RT in Piccadilly Circus. The key distinguishing feature of the 150 RT-Type AEC Regents delivered in 1939-40 was the downward curve on the lower edge of the windscreen.

London Transport
A BRIEF OVERVIEW

The London Passenger Transport Board – which traded as London Transport – was formed on 1 July 1933 and assumed responsibility for virtually all local bus, tram and trolleybus services in an area covering roughly a 30 mile radius from Charing Cross. It also took over the rail services provided by the Underground Electric Railways Group of companies and the Metropolitan Railway.

It was instrumental in setting high standards for public transport in and around the capital. Its early achievements included stylish new Underground stations served by modern trains – and the RT bus, perhaps the pinnacle of traditional half-cab bus design. It's hard to imagine how this stylish new bus was seen by people viewing prototype RT1 in 1939. Its low radiator and well-proportioned four-bay body set it apart from its contemporaries, the vast majority of which had tall radiators and five-bay bodies, the late 1930s standard for double-deck buses. The driver's cab had a distinctive deep windscreen and a sliding door.

The chassis of the RT was built by AEC, a company whose proud boast for many years was *Builders of London's Buses*. The London General Omnibus Co had started building buses at a factory in Walthamstow in 1909, and in 1912 formed the Associated Equipment Company as its bus-building arm. AEC became an independent business in 1933 when London General's bus operations were absorbed by the LPTB. AEC chassis manufacture had by then moved to a new purpose-built factory which had opened in Southall in 1927.

To maintain its growing fleet of motorbuses London General had opened a bus works at Chiswick in 1921. This not only overhauled buses, but also built bus bodies for London General and then London Transport from 1926 to 1941, plus a few prototypes after World War 2, notably the first two Routemasters. After the war LT developed a bus works at Aldenham in what was originally planned as a depot for Underground trains serving an extension of the Northern Line from Edgware to Bushey Heath. The line wasn't built, and in 1949 Aldenham started carrying out bus overhauls. The 54-acre site became fully operational in 1956 at which point it employed over 2,000 people. It was capable of turning out 56 overhauled vehicles every week at a time when LT's buses were overhauled every 3½ years.

LT's bus operations were divided into two areas. The Central Area's buses were red; those operated in the Country Area were green. There were in addition Green Line coach services which had been introduced by London General in 1930. The longest ran 55 miles from Hitchin to Reigate, taking 3 hours 30 minutes with an end-to-end single fare of five shillings (25p).

LONDON TRANSPORT'S AREA

The London Transport operating area as shown in LT's annual report in 1964. The boundary was little changed from that established when the London Passenger Transport Board was created in 1933.

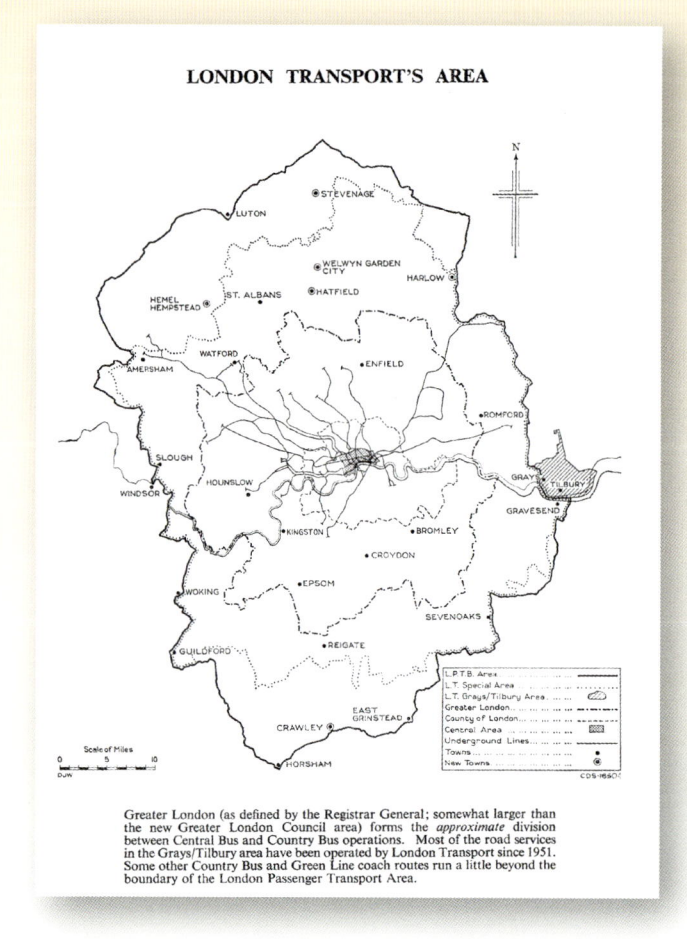

Greater London (as defined by the Registrar General; somewhat larger than the new Greater London Council area) forms the *approximate* division between Central Bus and Country Bus operations. Most of the road services in the Grays/Tilbury area have been operated by London Transport since 1951. Some other Country Bus and Green Line coach routes run a little beyond the boundary of the London Passenger Transport Area.

Along with its fleet of almost 6,000 motorbuses which it took over from 61 operators, LT acquired 2,630 trams (and 61 trolleybuses) operated by nine municipalities and three companies, ranging in size from London County Council with 1,663 trams to Erith Urban District Council with 19. The replacement of trams by trolleybuses got underway in 1935 and the aim was that the last trams would be withdrawn by 1943. By 1939 over 1,600 trolleybuses had been bought for tram replacement, but the outbreak of war disrupted LT's plans and the last trams did not come out of service until 1952. Most of the postwar trams were replaced not by trolleybuses but by diesel buses. LT's trolleybuses were in turn replaced by motorbuses between 1954 and 1962 with some of the newest operating in London for less than ten years.

The buses which replaced the 70-seat trolleybuses were, generally, 64-seat Routemasters. The integral Routemaster was the last bus to be designed by LT and was praised for its advanced design and low weight while being criticised for its unadventurous layout with its front engine and open rear platform.

No doubt aware of that criticism, it is worth noting the position of LT's chief mechanical engineer road services, A A M Durrant, as reported in *Commercial Motor* in the spring of 1958. This read: "A rear entrance without a door was selected to avoid loading and unloading delays, and at the same time provision of a rear staircase helped to

Aldenham Works was dedicated to the overhaul and repair of London's buses in a facility which was unmatched by any other British bus operator and, indeed, by many British bus manufacturers. Whether or not many other operators would actually want to separate bodies and chassis to carry out an overhaul is another matter. Here a Routemaster has had its running units removed; they will be overhauled separately and are unlikely to be reunited with the same body.

avoid congestion inside the bus. A front or central entrance would have had to have been fitted with a door for use in central London for safety reasons, and this would have slowed down passenger movements.

"There were several reasons for choosing a forward engine position: a rear engine would have reduced platform space, an underfloor engine carried amidships would have raised the floor and step heights, and in any case the space to the left of the driver had been proved to be unsuitable for passenger seating because of the danger of distracting the driver. Furthermore, a half cab gave better driving vision."

While the Transport & General Workers' Union, which represented platform staff, was prepared to see 64-seat Routemasters replace 70-seat trolleybuses, it was not happy about Routemasters replacing 56-seat RTs. There was a level of militancy among London bus crews which was not evidenced elsewhere in Britain where bigger buses replaced smaller ones with little adverse reaction from drivers or conductors.

So when the trolleybus replacement programme was nearing completion the union and its members dug their collective heels in, and Routemasters being delivered from July 1961 went in to storage rather than in to service. In October LT executive member Brian Harbour complained that 180 new buses worth £1million were standing idle. They started to enter service from November when LT agreed on a one-for-one replacement of RTs by Routemasters instead of using fewer Routemasters because they were bigger; seven RMs provided the same number of seats as eight RTs. There then followed further negotiations over the introduction of 72-seat Routemasters and the separate but no less contentious issue of one-man-operation.

These changes were taking place against a background of major challenges for the British bus industry. From the early 1950s there had been a steady decline in bus use as more and more people bought cars. More cars meant more congestion, making bus services less attractive. And in a period of full employment it became harder for LT to recruit drivers and conductors. LT's solution to these problems, set out in its Bus Reshaping Plan in 1966, was to design shorter suburban routes to be operated by one-man buses. The problem with long routes was that localised congestion at one end had a knock-on effect on the reliability of the entire route. While shorter routes would still be affected by congestion, the effects would be localised. And having the driver collect fares would reduce the need for conductors, ameliorating the staff shortage and reducing costs. Initially the one-man buses were rear-engined AEC single-deckers then from 1971 Daimler Fleetline double-deckers. Neither type could be described as an unqualified success.

A clever use for one-man buses in central London appeared in 1966 with the launch of the limited-stop Red Arrow service 500 between Victoria Station and Marble Arch with a flat fare

With just 25 seats the one-man-operated AEC single-deckers of the late 1960s had proved unpopular. Ealing area services E1 and E2 had been introduced in 1968 with Merlins. When they were replaced by double-deckers in 1975 LT emphasised that the new buses were offering more seats; the DMS Fleetlines had 68 seats.

of sixpence (2.5p). The service was such a success that a further seven routes, all serving mainline railway terminals, were introduced in 1968. The Red Arrow network had an allocation of 58 buses operated from three garages, Victoria, Hackney and Walworth.

Changing structures

The postwar Labour government supported the nationalisation of transport and under powers in the 1947 Transport Act the London Passenger Transport Board had been replaced by the state-owned London Transport Executive, which was part of the British Transport Commission. The 1962 Transport Act brought further change with the winding up of BTC, and the replacement at the start of 1963 of the London Transport Executive by the London Transport Board.

But it was the Transport (London) Act of 1969 which brought major change. LT's Country Area operations were taken over in January 1970 by a new subsidiary of the state-owned National Bus Company, London Country Bus Services, with its head office in Reigate. This saw the transfer from LT to NBC of 1,267 vehicles, including those used on Green Line services, along with 28 garages in Bedfordshire, Buckinghamshire, Essex, Hertfordshire, Kent, Middlesex, Surrey and Sussex. The LCBS fleet was elderly, and included around 900 RTs and RFs, all over 15 years old; the only modern vehicles were AEC Merlins, of which there were just over 100.

At the same time London's Underground and red bus services were placed under the control of the Greater London Council, which had been created in 1965. The organisation reverted to its pre-1963 title of the London Transport Executive, running almost 6,200 buses from 68 garages.

One of LT's last high-profile initiatives was an adaptation of the concept of the Red Arrow express service to a commuter route in Stevenage. This was the Blue Arrow, linking the Chells residential suburb with the town's industrial area and offering something akin to a door-to-door service for workers. It was promoted as "Bus to work taxi-style". The service was started by LT on 29 December 1969 and was then taken over by London Country three days later.

From the early 1980s the then Labour-controlled GLC increasingly came into direct confrontation with the Conservative-controlled central government – often over transport issues. In the end the government decided there was only one way to solve the problems it had with the GLC: abolish it.

This meant a new owner had to be created for London's bus and Underground systems, and this was addressed by the 1984 London Regional Transport Act which set up London Regional Transport to take over the GLC-owned London Transport Executive.

Under the Act four LRT subsidiary companies came into being on 1 April 1985 – London Buses Ltd, London Underground Ltd, the consultancy business London Transport International Services Ltd, and Bus Engineering Ltd, which took over the bus works at Chiswick and Aldenham. The long-term aim, in keeping with the thinking of the Conservative government, was that these companies would be sold to the private sector. London's bus fleet in 1985 was considerably smaller than it had been three decades earlier, and newer types of vehicles did not fit in comfortably (or at all) with Aldenham's methods of working. Aldenham closed in 1986 with some of its functions being transferred to Chiswick Works. Bus Engineering Ltd was privatised in 1988 when it was sold to Frontsource, a business formed in the previous year to buy NBC's eight engineering companies.

The newly-formed London Buses Ltd claimed to be the biggest bus operator in Western Europe. Its fleet numbered some 5,500 buses which carried over 3.5 million people a day. Its annual turnover was almost £440million. London Buses had 57 garages and employed

24,200 people of whom 12,800 were drivers and 4,700 were conductors. The 5,500 buses covered 172 million miles a year and consumed 23 million gallons of diesel. A quick tap on the buttons of a calculator will show that equates to an average fuel consumption of 7.5mpg. At this time virtually all of London's buses were full-size heavy-duty models, and most were double-deckers.

The 1984 Act required LRT to put London's bus routes out for competitive tender, with the first tenders being awarded in 1985. Just over half of the early tenders were won by independent operators, and in 1986 London Buses created two subsidiaries in which the staff were employed on lower wage rates with different working agreements. This was done to cut costs and be better able to compete with the new breed of independent operators who had lower overheads. The two subsidiares were Stanwell Buses Ltd, which traded as Westlink, and Orpington Buses Ltd, trading as Roundabout. Both were successful in winning LRT contracts.

Also established in 1986, in January, was the Commercial Operations Unit initially with just three coaches. Later in the year it adopted the rather catchier London Coaches as its trading name. Within five years it would be running over 100 vehicles. Part of its expansion came in 1988 when it took over commuter services linking North Kent and London which had previously been operated by Bexleyheath Transport.

The tendering regime had a major impact on the London Buses fleet. In each year between 1970 and 1986 an average of just over 300 new double-deckers joined the London fleet. Then over the seven years from 1987 to 1993 a *total* of only 255 new 'deckers were purchased. London Buses was instead buying small buses, starting with Mercedes-Benz midibuses and ending with Dennis Darts.

Yet there was still interest in alternatives, most notably at Selkent which tried two high-capacity vehicles in 1992. First was a new three-axle Leyland Olympian with 96-seat air-conditioned Alexander body which was destined for Hong Kong Citybus. The second was the first articulated bus to operate in service in London, a seven-year-old three-door Leyland DAB borrowed from South Yorkshire Transport. It could carry an impressive 144 passengers, with seats for 61 of them. Both buses operated on the 180 between Abbey Wood and Catford.

When local bus services in Great Britain outside London had been deregulated in 1986, the government stated that London's bus services would be deregulated in the early 1990s.

1989 reorganisation

Company	Fleet	Garages
CentreWest London Buses	405	Alperton, Hanwell, Uxbridge, Westbourne Park
East London Bus & Coach Co	536	Barking, Bow, Romford, Seven Kings, Upton Park, West Ham
Leaside Bus Company	424	Enfield, Palmers Green, Stamford Hill, Tottenham, Wood Green
London Central Bus Co	418	Camberwell, New Cross, Peckham
London Forest Travel	361	Ash Grove, Leyton, Walthamstow
London General Transport Services	582	Merton, Putney, Red Arrow base, Stockwell, Sutton, Victoria
London Northern Bus Co	379	Chalk Farm, Finchley, Holloway, Muswell Hill, Potters Bar
London United Busways	433	Fulwell, Hounslow, Norbiton, Shepherds Bush, Stamford Brook
Metroline Travel	343	Cricklewood, Edgware, Harrow, Willesden
South East London & Kent Bus Co	461	Bexleyheath, Bromley, Catford, Orpington, Plumstead
South London Transport	455	Brixton, Croydon, Norwood, Streatham, Thornton Heath

Of the two limited companies set up in 1986, Stanwell Buses remained as a separate business, but Orpington Buses became part of Selkent. London Forest was disbanded in 1991 following a 19-day strike over pay and conditions.

The first articulated bus to run in service in London was Leyland-DAB C101 HDT, borrowed by Selkent from South Yorkshire Transport in 1992. The bus was built in Denmark and had a 245bhp Leyland TL11H engine mounted under the floor of the front section and a ZF automatic gearbox. It carries Selkent fleetnames and a London Buses roundel on the side. Tony Wilson

The government's commitment to deregulation in London was confirmed periodically by a succession of transport ministers and in February 1992 the aim was for deregulation sometime around 1994, to be followed by privatisation around 1995. But politicians are not always noted for keeping promises and London's bus services were never opened up to the on-street competition seen in other British cities.

In readiness for privatisation a major reorganisation in 1989 saw the creation of 11 operating units, each with its own management team, as shown in the panel opposite. With the formation of the new companies the legal lettering on the sides of the vehicles changed. After over 50 years of displaying 55 Broadway as the address of London Transport in its various forms, London's buses now displayed the sometimes obscure suburban addresses of the operating subsidiaries.

The privatisation of London Buses got underway in 1992 with a management buy-out at London Coaches, then gathered pace in 1994, as shown in the list below. Six companies were the subject of management buy-outs while the remainder were bought by Stagecoach, Cowie, Go-Ahead and MTL.

Perth-based Stagecoach was at this time Britain's biggest bus company and was expanding rapidly. The two London companies which it bought ran 1,000 buses between them, and increased Stagecoach's UK fleet to some 6,000 vehicles.

Cowie, with its headquarters in Sunderland, was primarily involved in the motor trade, but had owned London coach operator Grey-Green since 1981 so had experience of London bus operation under the LRT tendering regime. It also owned the Hughes DAF coach dealership in Yorkshire, which it purchased in 1987. Go-Ahead, a former NBC management buy-out, was based in Gateshead and had extensive experience of urban bus operation in the north-east of England. MTL was the private sector successor to the Merseyside PTE's bus operation and had a fleet of 1,000 buses in Liverpool and its hinterland so, like Go-Ahead, was no stranger to intensive urban bus services.

London Buses had changed dramatically since it was formed in 1985. At that time it had around 5,500 buses and 24,200 employees, which equals 4.4 employees per bus. By 1994 the fleet had dropped to 4,800 vehicles, while the number of employees had fallen by over 9,000 to 15,494, or just 3.2 employees per bus. The number of employees per bus can be translated as a rough measure of efficiency; the lower the figure, the more efficient the operation.

Equally significantly, the organisation no longer subscribed to what had once seemed to be its dictum: "If we didn't design it, it won't work in London." From bespoke RTs and Routemasters to hydraulically-braked Leyland Titans and MCW Metrobuses London Transport had for over 40 years exercised varying degrees of control over the design of the buses it was buying. Then, just five years after the last Titan was delivered in 1984, London Buses was buying new buses from dealers' or manufacturers' stock.

And, of course, they worked.

The privatisation programme

Date	Company	Fleet	New owner
May 1992	London Coaches	109	Management buy-out
January 1994	Westlink	118	Management buy-out
September 1994	CentreWest	507	Management buy-out
	East London	592	Stagecoach
	Selkent	414	Stagecoach
	Leaside	523	Cowie
October 1994	Metroline	386	Management buy-out
	London Central	498	Go-Ahead
	London Northern	341	MTL
	London General	636	Management buy-out
November 1994	London United	464	Management buy-out
January 1995	South London	447	Cowie

At a glance

London Transport road fleet

	1944	1956	1960	1970	1980	1990	2019
Motorbuses	6,389	8,404	7,743	6,194	6,481	4,915	9,300
Trolleybuses	1,411	1,764	723	-	-	-	-
Trams	1,316	-	-	-	-	-	-
Total	**9,116**	**10,168**	**8,466**	**6,194**	**6,481**	**4,915**	**9,300**

Source: *Passenger Transport Year Book* (1944, 1956, 1960); *The Little Red Book* (1970, 1980, 1990); *Transport for London* (2019, for comparison)

London's green buses

Vehicles delivered in Green Line livery, 1945–1965

Type	Chassis	Year	Quantity
D	Daimler CWA6	1945-46	37
RTC	AEC Regent	1949	1
RT	AEC Regent III	1950-54	57
RF	AEC Regal IV	1951-52	263
CRL	Routemaster	1957	1
RMC	Routemaster	1962	68
RCL	Routemaster	1965	43
RC	AEC Reliance	1965	14
Total			**484**

Vehicles delivered in Country Area green livery, 1946–1971

Type	Chassis	Year	Quantity
STL	AEC Regent	1946	20
T	AEC Regal III	1948	30
RLH	AEC Regent III	1950-52	52
RT	AEC Regent III	1948-54	621
RF	AEC Regal IV	1953	187
GS	Guy Special	1953	84
RM	Routemaster	1955	1
RML	Routemaster	1965-66	100
RW	AEC Reliance	1960	3
TT	Thames 570E	1963	5
XF	Daimler Fleetline	1965	8
MB	AEC Merlin	1966-68	118
SM	AEC Swift	1970-71	138
Total			**1,367**

The AEC Swifts were ordered by LT but delivered to London Country Bus Services.

OVERLEAF: The changing face of London's buses as illustrated on the cover of the 1989 Central Bus Guide.

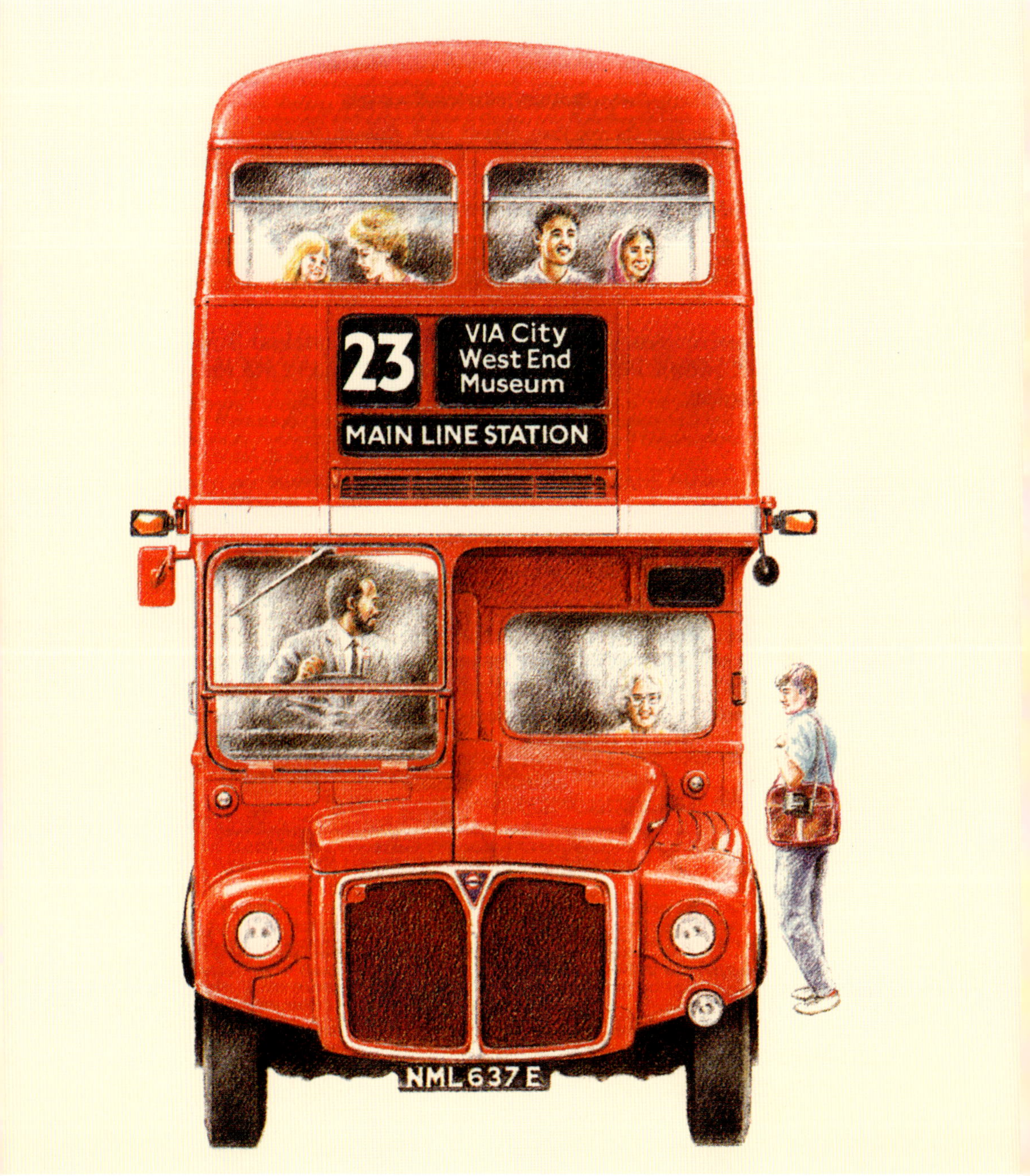
23
VIA City
West End
Museum
MAIN LINE STATION
NML 637 E

London Transport's bus purchases

Wartime classes

From 1942 to 1945 there were tight controls by the Ministry of Supply on the manufacture of new buses, and by the Ministry of War Transport of their allocation to operators as the government directed industrial production to support the war effort. Just three manufacturers were authorised to produce double-deck bus chassis during the war, Bristol, Daimler and Guy, and these were fitted with bodies built to utility standards which had been set by the Ministry of Supply in the autumn of 1941. This conserved scarce materials and minimised the use of skilled labour. Steel replaced aluminium for most of the exterior panelling, and for much of the war slatted wooden seats – offering all the comfort of a garden bench – were fitted to new buses.

The first of London's wartime Guys in 1942 were Park Royal-bodied Arab Is, such as G19 at Victoria. The Arab I had a five-cylinder Gardner 5LW engine, as did all of London's Arab IIs although six-cylinder versions were provided to operators elsewhere in Britain. Lodge was a Rugby-based manufacturer of spark plugs for petrol engines.

London Transport's first new Bristols, in 1942, were nine Gardner-engined K5Gs with prewar-style high radiators and Park Royal utility bodywork. B5 is in Perivale in 1952 on service 97, Ruislip to Brentford.

London Transport received new Bristols and Guys from 1942, followed by Daimlers in 1944-46. The first of the Bristols and all of the wartime Guys had 85bhp Gardner five-cylinder engines, while a second batch of Bristols in 1946 and most of the Daimlers had more powerful 95bhp AEC engines. Daimler's new 100bhp CD6 engine was fitted to 13 CWD6 chassis in 1945-46. In total there were 745 of these wartime buses, 435 Guys, 281 Daimlers and 29 Bristols.

Bodywork was supplied by seven builders. Park Royal Coachworks of NW10 and Weymann of Addlestone in Surrey had built buses for LT in the 1930s and between them supplied 366 bodies on Bristol and Guy chassis, making up almost half of London's wartime body deliveries. The others were new suppliers to LT: Duple Motor Bodies of Hendon (128 bodies), Northern Counties Motor & Engineering Co of Wigan (102), Brush Electrical Engineering Co of Loughborough (74), Massey Brothers of Wigan (49) and Northern Coachbuilders of Newcastle upon Tyne (26 plus one rebody). The 26 Northern Coachbuilders bodies supplied on new Guy chassis in 1945 were subcontracted from Park Royal and built to Park Royal's designs.

The first 50 Guys were delivered in 1942, and were followed by another 50 in 1943. Guys, in ever increasing quantities, would enter the fleet until 1946. The last of the Guys were withdrawn in 1952; many saw further service elsewhere, from Caithness to Ceylon. Major buyers of LT's redundant Guys were the Scottish Omnibuses group with 129 and Edinburgh Corporation with 60 which were fitted with new bodies before entering service.

The nine Gardner-engined K5Gs delivered in 1942 were London Transport's first new Bristols. The 20 which followed in 1946 were of an improved design with a lower radiator and AEC engines. The Bristols operated from Hanwell garage, and the K5Gs were fitted with AEC engines in 1949 in the interests of standardisation. All 29 Bristols were sold to companies in the state-owned Tilling Group in 1953 – Crosville Motor Services (14), Lincolnshire Road Car (seven), and four each to Brighton Hove & District and United Automobile Services.

There had been Daimler buses operating in London from Edwardian times, and in 1930 London General had purchased three (creating a DST class) to evaluate their preselector gearboxes. The next Daimlers were the wartime allocations in 1944, and by 1946 there were

281 Daimlers in service with LT. Merton garage was the home of most of the red-liveried Daimlers, including the ten with side-gangway lowbridge bodies for route 127 (Morden Station to South Wimbledon Station) which passed under a low bridge at Worcester Park Station. These buses were replaced by RLH-class AEC Regents in 1952. There were 37 Duple-bodied buses which were new in Green Line livery and initially operated from Romford garage on routes 721 and 722 to Aldgate from Brentwood and Upminster respectively. They were replaced by RTs in 1950. The last 100 Daimlers in 1946, bodied by Park Royal, were allocated to Sutton garage. Belfast Corporation Transport bought 100 of LT's CWA6s in 1953 and 89 were exported to Ceylon. The last in London service were withdrawn at the start of 1954.

Specifications

Model	Engine	Displacement	Power output	Gearbox
Bristol K5G	Gardner 5LW	7 litres	85bhp	Bristol four-speed constant mesh
Bristol K6A	AEC A202	7.7 litres	95bhp	Bristol four-speed constant mesh
Daimler CWA6	AEC A173	7.7 litres	95bhp	Daimler four-speed preselector
Daimler CWD6	Daimler CD6	8.6 litres	100bhp	Daimler four-speed preselector
Guy Arab	Gardner 5LW	7 litres	85bhp	Guy four-speed manual

B Bristol K

B1-9	FXT 419-427	Bristol K5G	Park Royal H30/26R	1942
B10-29	HGC 235-254	Bristol K6A	Duple H30/26R	1945-46

D Daimler CW-series

The 37 buses highlighted in green were new in Green Line livery.
They were replaced by 36 RTs (RT3224–3259) in 1950.

D1-6	GXE 578-583	Daimler CWA6	Duple L27/28R	1944
D7-13	GXE 584-590	Daimler CWA6	Duple H30/26R	1944
D14-34	GLX 900-920	Daimler CWA6	Duple H30/26R	1944
D35-38	GLX 921-924	Daimler CWA6	Brush H30/26R	1945
D39-61	GXV 770-792	Daimler CWA6	Brush H30/26R	1945
D62-73	GYE 51-62	Daimler CWA6	Brush H30/26R	1945
D74-92	GYE 64-82	Daimler CWA6	Duple H30/26R	1945
D93-95	GYE 98-100	Daimler CWA6	Brush H30/26R	1945
D96-126	GYL 261-291	Daimler CWA6	Brush H30/26R	1945
D127	GYL 292	Daimler CWD6	Brush H30/26R	1945
D128-131	HGC 255-258	Daimler CWA6	Duple L27/28R	1945
D132	HGC 259	Daimler CWA6	Duple H30/26R	1945
D133-137	HGC 260-264	Daimler CWA6	Duple H30/26R	1945
D138-140	HGC 265-267	Daimler CWD6	Duple H30/26R	1945
D141	HGC 268	Daimler CWA6	Duple H30/26R	1945
D142	HGC 269	Daimler CWD6	Duple H30/26R	1945
D143-149	HGC 270-276	Daimler CWA6	Duple H30/26R	1946
D150	HGC 277	Daimler CWD6	Duple H30/26R	1946
D151-154	HGC 278-281	Daimler CWA6	Duple H30/26R	1946
D155	HGC 282	Daimler CWD6	Duple H30/26R	1946
D156-159	HGC 283-286	Daimler CWA6	Duple H30/26R	1946
D160	HGC 287	Daimler CWD6	Duple H30/26R	1946

LT's first Daimler CWA6s in 1944 were half a dozen with lowbridge Duple bodies. They were based at Morden for a service which passed under a low bridge at Worcester Park Station. D1 shows the protective screening applied to the windows of some wartime buses to prevent passengers being injured by splinters of glass in the event of a bomb exploding nearby. The white edges on the front mudguards were intended to make the vehicle more visible during a blackout. *E G Masterman/The Bus Archive*

Daimler CWA6 D69 negotiates Parliament Square in the summer of 1952 after being repainted in all-over red with just a thin cream relief band; previously it would have been in the more attractive livery with white window surrounds shown on D1 above. The body was by Brush of Loughborough. Among the products offered by Ediswan are television tubes and radio valves.

D161	HGC 288	Daimler CWA6	Duple H30/26R	1946
D162-163	HGC 289-290	Daimler CWD6	Duple H30/26R	1946
D164-170	HGC 291-297	Daimler CWA6	Duple H30/26R	1946
D171	HGC 298	Daimler CWD6	Duple H30/26R	1946
D172	HGC 299	Daimler CWA6	Duple H30/26R	1946
D173-179	HGF 800-806	Daimler CWA6	Duple H30/26R	1946
D180-181	HGF 807-808	Daimler CWD6	Duple H30/26R	1946
D182-281	HGF 859-958	Daimler CWA6	Park Royal H30/26R	1946

G Guy Arab

G1-31	GLF 651-681	Guy Arab I	Park Royal H30/26R	1942
G32-42	GLF 682-692	Guy Arab I	Weymann H30/26R	1942
G43	GLF 693	Guy Arab I	Duple H30/26R	1942
G44-50	GLF 694-700	Guy Arab I	Weymann H30/26R	1942
G51-71	GLL 551-571	Guy Arab I	Park Royal H30/26R	1943
G72-84	GLL 572-584	Guy Arab II	Park Royal H30/26R	1943
G85	GLL 600	Guy Arab II	Park Royal H30/26R	1943
G86-100	GLL 585-599	Guy Arab II	Park Royal H30/26R	1943
G101-136	GXE 541-576	Guy Arab II	Park Royal H30/26R	1944
G137-138	GXV 793-794	Guy Arab II	Weymann H30/26R	1945
G139-149	GYE 83-93	Guy Arab II	Northern Coachbuilders H30/26R	1945
G150	GYE 94	Guy Arab II	Park Royal H30/26R	1945
G151-153	GYE 95-97	Guy Arab II	Northern Coachbuilders H30/26R	1945
G154-173	GYL 293-312	Guy Arab II	Northern Counties H30/26R	1945
G174-193	GYL 313-332	Guy Arab II	Massey H30/26R	1945
G194-205	GYL 333-344	Guy Arab II	Northern Coachbuilders H30/26R	1945
G206-218	GYL 345-357	Guy Arab II	Park Royal H30/26R	1945
G219-257	GYL 358-396	Guy Arab II	Northern Counties H30/26R	1945
G258-268	GYL 397-407	Guy Arab II	Massey H30/26R	1945
G269-311	GYL 409-451	Guy Arab II	Northern Counties H30/26R	1945-46
G312-318	GYL 452-458	Guy Arab II	Massey H30/26R	1945
G319-320	GYL 459-460	Guy Arab II	Park Royal H30/26R	1945
G321-357	HGC 100-136	Guy Arab II	Park Royal H30/26R	1945-46
G358-368	HGC 137-147	Guy Arab II	Massey H30/26R	1945
G369-430	HGC 148-209	Guy Arab II	Weymann H30/26R	1945
G431-435	HGC 210-214	Guy Arab II	Park Royal H30/26R	1946
G436	KGK 981	Guy Arab III see page 30		

● G30 rebodied by Northern Coachbuilders in 1944, after being damaged by a bomb.

The first postwar Green Line vehicles were 37 Daimler CWA6s. *W J Wyse*

Non-standard deliveries 1946-53

London Transport had before the outbreak of war in 1939 developed what would become its standard postwar bus, the RT – see page 35. But when the war ended it needed to expedite the delivery of new buses and to this end 65 Leyland Titan PD1s and 20 AEC Regent IIs to their respective manufacturers' standard specifications were purchased in 1946. The Regents were the Country Area's first new double-deckers since 1936 and were originally based at Watford. The Regents had Weymann bodies while the Titans were bodied in Leyland's own workshops. Both bodybuilders' products were to their standard

STD112, the first of London's Leyland Titan PD1s, was photographed in Leyland before making the 200-mile delivery trip south. Leyland's standard body has a few London features, the most obvious being the roof-mounted route number box and the lower-deck side panels which are in two parts with a horizontal moulding strip covering the join. An odd collection of destination and route number blinds has been gathered for the photograph, showing route numbers 442, 76 and 25B. *British Commercial Vehicle Museum*

postwar designs. All 65 PD1s were exported to Yugoslavia in 1955. The 20 Regents were sold in 1955 to three municipal fleets – Dundee (ten), Widnes (six) and Grimsby (four).

There was also an urgent need for new single-deckers after the war and in 1946-47 LT received 50 AEC Regals and 31 Leyland Tigers with Weymann bodies. These were the single-deck equivalents of the Regent IIs and Titan PD1s being delivered around the same time. In 1948 these were followed by further 30 Regals for Country Area services, now Mark III models with the bigger and more powerful 9.6-litre engine which powered the RT-type double-deckers; the earlier Regals and Regents had 7.7-litre engines. There were also 100 more Leyland Tigers. The bodies for these 130 buses were built by Mann Egerton of Norwich. The 30 Country Area buses had a sliding door for the passenger entrance; the 181 for the Central Area had no door. Most of the Tigers – 98 – were sold to Ceylon at the end of the 1950s. The last in LT service were withdrawn in 1962, bringing to an end the operation by LT of half-cab single-deckers.

Additional standard AEC Regent chassis – the improved Mark III – were delivered in 1950 and 1952 and were fitted with side-gangway lowbridge Weymann bodies, with a nominal height of 13ft 3in compared with 14ft 3in for an RT. This enabled them to pass under bridges with limited overhead clearance. They were London's only postwar lowbridge buses. The first 20 were a diverted Midland General order. Midland General, like LT, was a subsidiary of the British Transport Commission. The last lowbridge Regents were withdrawn in 1971 and replaced by AEC Swifts.

The other non-standard double-decker was a solitary Guy Arab III which had a Meadows 6DC430 engine and a preselector gearbox and was supplied by its manufacturer in the hope of securing orders from London Transport. It didn't, although LT would turn to Guy in 1953 when it needed a new fleet of small single-deck buses for Country Area services. The Arab III was exported to Yugoslavia in 1955. Guy had intended to build a second Arab III for LT with a chassis frame similar to that of an RT-class AEC Regent, but this was not proceeded with.

The first new postwar Country Area buses were 20 Weymann-bodied AEC Regent IIs in 1946. STL2692 and three others are ready for service at Garston garage in 1953. When they were new the livery was brighter, with white window surrounds on both decks. All 20 of the postwar STLs were withdrawn in 1955.

LT's first 50 postwar AEC Regals in 1946 were O662 models with 7.7-litre engines and manual gearboxes. The attractive lines of the Weymann body were marred by the deep destination box which covered the top section of the windscreen. T742 is in Kingston. Weymann supplied 31 similar bodies on Leyland Tiger chassis. These Regals were sold between 1954 and 1958, with 28 seeing further service in Ceylon.

The pretty little GS class buses were based on a chassis developed by Guy to meet LT's requirements for a replacement for its fleet of pre-war Leyland Cubs used on lightly-loaded Country Area routes. The GS used an Otter chassis converted to normal control and fitted with Vixen axles and springs to give a better ride. The buses were 25ft long and 7ft 6in wide and had Eastern Coach Works bodies with 26 seats, the maximum capacity permitted for one-man operation in 1953. The bonnet and front wing assembly was produced by Briggs Motor Bodies of Dagenham and was adapted from that used on some contemporary lorries such as the Fordson Thames ET6. ECW, based in Lowestoft, was at this time a state-owned business with its sales restricted to other state-owned operators.

The Guy chassis type was NLLVDP, indicating **N**ormal control, **L**ong, **L**ong (wheelbase lengthened by 3in over the standard) **V**ixen **D**iesel **P**erkins. The P6 engine was manufactured in Peterborough and was a 4.7-litre six-cylinder unit.

Specifications

Model	Engine	Displacement	Power	Gearbox
AEC Regal	AEC A173	7.7 litres	95bhp	AEC four-speed constant-mesh
AEC Regal III	AEC A208	9.6 litres	125bhp	AEC four-speed preselector
AEC Regent II	AEC A173	7.7 litres	95bhp	AEC four-speed constant-mesh
AEC Regent III	AEC A208	9.6 litres	115bhp	AEC four-speed preselector
Guy Arab III	Meadows 6DC430	10.35 litres	130bhp	Guy four-speed preselector
Guy Vixen Special	Perkins P6	4.7 litres	65bhp	Guy four-speed constant-mesh
Leyland Tiger PS1	Leyland E181	7.4 litres	100bhp	Leyland four-speed constant mesh
Leyland Titan PD1	Leyland E181	7.4 litres	100bhp	Leyland four-speed constant mesh

STD Leyland Titan PD1

| STD112-121 | HGF 990-999 | Leyland Titan PD1 | Leyland H30/26R | 1946 |
| STD122-176 | HLW 51-105 | Leyland Titan PD1 | Leyland H30/26R | 1946 |

STL AEC Regent II

| STL2682-2701 | HGC 215-234 | AEC Regent II O661 | Weymann H30/26R | 1946 |

- These were Country Area buses.

T AEC Regal

| T719-768 | HGF 809-858 | AEC Regal O662 | Weymann B35F | 1946 |
| T769-798 | HLX 439-468 | AEC Regal III 9621E | Mann Egerton B31F | 1948 |

- T769-798 were Country Area buses. Some of the early chassis were O962 models, but all were built to the same specification.

TD Leyland Tiger PS1

| TD1-31 | HGF 959-989 | Leyland Tiger PS1 | Weymann B33F | 1946-47 |
| TD32-131 | JXC 225-324 | Leyland Tiger PS1 | Mann Egerton B31F | 1948-49 |

G Guy Arab III

| G436 | KGK 981 | Guy Arab III | Park Royal H30/26R | 1949 |

Leyland Tiger TD90 was one of 100 with bodywork by Mann Egerton of Norwich. Similar bodies were fitted to 30 Country Area AEC Regal IIIs. The driver's cab had a sliding door, an unusual feature to find on a single-deck bus. The Tiger is preparing to overtake a prewar Y-series Ford in Winchmore Hill with the Green Dragon pub on the right; the pub building survives as a branch of Waitrose.

The last of the early postwar non-standard double-deckers were the 76 RLH class AEC Regent IIIs with lowbridge Weymann bodies. Country Area RLH14 was new in 1950 and is seen in Staines in 1967. It was taken over by London Country in January 1970 and withdrawn later that year. *Geoffrey Morant*

RLH AEC Regent III

RLH1-20	KYY 501-520	AEC Regent III 9612E	Weymann L27/26R	1950
RLH21-52	MXX 221-252	AEC Regent III 9613E	Weymann L27/26R	1952
RLH53-76	MXX 253-276	AEC Regent III 9613E	Weymann L27/26R	1952

- RLH1-52 were Country Area buses.

GS Guy Vixen special

| GS1-84 | MXX 301-384 | Guy Special | ECW B26F | 1953 |

- These were Country Area buses.

GS35 in Windsor on the short service to Datchet illustrates the neat appearance of the little buses which Guy developed specifically for LT. The 26-seat body was by ECW. *Geoffrey Morant*

G436 was the last Guy Arab for LT. It had a Park Royal body and was delivered in 1949 and operated until 1955. When new it was allocated to Peckham garage for short route 173, the Peckham to Nunhead circular. It was the only Meadows-engined bus in the postwar LT fleet.

BUT trolleybuses

Trolleybuses were introduced to London in May 1931 by London United Tramways which used 60 to replace trams on routes centred on Kingston upon Thames. By the early 1950s the LT trolleybus fleet numbered around 1,800 vehicles, making it easily the biggest in the world. The next largest was Chicago, with just over 700. LT had used trolleybuses to replace trams in the late 1930s, and most were high-capacity three-axle double-deckers. The same layout was used for the 127 postwar additions to the fleet, the Q1 class. These were supplied by British United Traction, an amalgamation in 1946 of the trolleybus manufacturing activities of AEC and Leyland. BUT double-deck chassis were usually produced at the AEC factory in Southall but the 50 delivered to London in 1952 were assembled at the Crossley factory in Stockport. Crossley was a sister company of AEC. The Metro-Cammell bodies were a development of a style first seen on London trolleybuses in 1935. The Q1s were allocated to former London United depots at Fulwell, Hanwell and Isleworth.

When the decision was announced in 1954 that London's trolleybuses would be replaced by diesel buses the system covered 253 route miles and carried 750 million passengers a year, accounting for 20 per cent of LT's road passengers. The Q1s were withdrawn in 1960-61, with 125 being sold to operators in Spain. London's last trolleybuses ran in May 1962.

| 1765-1841 | HYM 765-841 | BUT 9641T | Metro-Cammell H40/30R | 1948-49 |
| 1842-1891 | LYH 842-891 | BUT 9641T | Metro-Cammell H40/30R | 1952 |

A 1950 advert for Tecalemit chassis lubrication featured this attractive illustration of Metro-Cammell-bodied BUT trolleybus 1779. It is based on a black-and-white photograph.

The RT family

The prototype of London Transport's new standard double-decker, the RT-class AEC Regent, was unveiled in 1939. An initial batch of 150 entered service in 1940-41 with bodies built in Chiswick Works. When volume production got under way after World War 2, the highly-standardised RT-type body was built not at Chiswick, but by outside contractors. Large numbers were produced by Park Royal, Metro-Cammell and Weymann, and smaller quantities by Saunders Engineering & Shipyard of Anglesey (300) and Cravens of Sheffield (120). The Cravens bodies were based on the company's five-bay body structure and were quite clearly different from the standard four-bay RT. Being non-standard they were

RT2337 swings in to Parliament Square in 1961, on a warm day to judge by the open windows. When new in 1949 it had a standard Weymann body but by 1961 had been fitted with a body with a roof-mounted route number display. *Iain MacGregor*

You have to admire the skills of colourists and re-touch artists. For its advertising in the early 1950s Park Royal created composite pictures to produce attractive scenes such as this showing RT1830 on route 11 in Parliament Square. The background is a black-and-white photograph which has been hand-coloured. The RT would also have started out as a black-and-white photo, probably of a brand new bus at the Park Royal factory which would explain the absence of adverts. The artist has added colour and passengers.

among the first RTs to be withdrawn in the mid 1950s and over half of them found new homes in Scotland, including 30 bought by Dundee Corporation Transport.

In addition to the 4,825 AEC Regents which formed the RT class, there were also 2,131 broadly similar Leyland Titan PD2s comprising 1,631 RTLs plus 500 RTWs which were LT's first 8ft-wide motorbuses. Most of the RTLs were bodied by Park Royal, but there were 450 with Metro-Cammell bodies built in Birmingham and 32 which were bodied by Weymann. All of the bodies on the 8ft-wide RTWs were built by Leyland. The RTs had 9.6-litre AEC engines while the RTLs and RTWs had Leyland's 9.8-litre O.600, the 600 figure being the engine's displacement in cubic inches. The Metropolitan Police was unhappy about 8ft-wide buses running in central London, and the first RTWs entered service in the suburbs. After a series of experimental conversions of central area services it was agreed in 1950 that they could operate anywhere except on roads where trams were still running.

Total production of AEC Regent IIIs was just under 8,400, with London's RTs accounting for well over half.

In the late 1940s it was becoming clear that new bodies were going be built faster than new chassis. LT then embarked on a major rebuild at Aldenham Works of 160 pre-war STL-class Regents which were fitted with new Park Royal RT-type bodies in 1949, creating the SRT class. These had 95bhp 7.7-litre engines and in consequence were underpowered when compared with genuine RT s which had 115bhp engines. The bodies on the SRTs were transferred to new RT chassis in 1953-54.

A key feature of the RT family was standardisation, and when vehicles were given major overhauls at Aldenham Works the bodies and chassis were separated. This meant that when the work was completed the overhauled chassis would usually be fitted with a different body from that which it had carried when it entered the works. LT claimed in 1952 that on average an RT would cover 40,000 miles without a mechanical failure and that fuel consumption was 9.5mpg.

The RTs replaced not only prewar and wartime buses, but also most of the 1,300 trams in service when World War 2 ended. But LT had over-estimated its requirements for new buses, not anticipating the inexorable decline in public transport use from the beginning of the 1950s as a growing number of people started buying cars and television sets. The family car had a direct impact on bus use while TV had an indirect impact as it hit cinema attendance. So when the last new RTs and RTLs were delivered in 1954 a total of 129 were put in to store as superfluous to requirements, with the last not entering passenger service until 1959, just before the first production Routemasters.

Most of the RTs were red Central Area buses but 621 were delivered in Country Area green, and a further 57 were new in Green Line livery. All of the Leylands were new in red, although 18 RTLs were repainted green in 1960 and operated from Hatfield garage for a short time.

Apart from the lowbridge RLH class of AEC Regents and the prototype Routemasters, all of the double-deck motorbuses in LT service between 1954 and 1958 were members of the RT family, a remarkable level of standardisation.

The last RTW was withdrawn from passenger service in 1966, followed by the last RTL in 1968, bringing an end to Leyland operation by LT until the delivery of the first of the new generation of Titans in 1978 (discounting the Leyland-badged Fleetlines of 1976-78). The RT was a remarkably long-lived type with the last being taken out of service in 1979 – at the same time as the first of the considerably younger DMS Fleetlines.

Specifications

Model	Engine	Displacement	Power output	Gearbox
AEC Regent SRT	AEC A173	7.7 litres	95bhp	AEC four-speed preselector
AEC Regent RT1-151	AEC A185	9.6 litres	100bhp	AEC four-speed preselector
AEC Regent III RT	AEC A204	9.6 litres	115bhp	AEC four-speed preselector
Leyland Titan PD2	Leyland O.600	9.8 litres	115bhp	AEC four-speed preselector

RT AEC Regent

The vehicles highlighted in green were Country Area buses, except RT3224-3259 and RT4489-4509 which were Green Line coaches.

RT1	EYK 396	AEC Regent	LPTB H29/26R (1939)	1938
RT2-151	FXT 177-326	AEC Regent	LPTB H30/26R	1940-41
RT152-263	HLW 139-250	AEC Regent III	Park Royal H30/26R	1947
RT264-401	HLX 81-218	AEC Regent III	Park Royal H30/26R	1948
RT402-596	HLX 219-413	AEC Regent III	Weymann H30/26R	1947-48
RT597-621	HLX 414-438	AEC Regent III	Weymann H30/26R	1948
RT622-651	JXC 430-459	AEC Regent III	Weymann H30/26R	1948
RT652-656	JXC 15-19	AEC Regent III	Park Royal H30/26R	1948
RT657	KLB 712	AEC Regent III	Park Royal H30/26R	1950
RT658-801	JXC 21-164	AEC Regent III	Park Royal H30/26R	1948
RT802-934	JXN 180-312	AEC Regent III	Park Royal H30/26R	1948
RT935-942	JXN 325-332	AEC Regent III	Park Royal H30/26R	1948
RT943	JXN 343	AEC Regent III	Park Royal H30/26R	1948
RT944-945	JXN 345-346	AEC Regent III	Park Royal H30/26R	1948
RT946-957	KGK 917-928	AEC Regent III	Park Royal H30/26R	1949
RT958-961	KGU 232-235	AEC Regent III	Park Royal H30/26R	1949
RT962-972	JXC 490-500	AEC Regent III	Weymann H30/26R	1948
RT973-1106	JXN 1-134	AEC Regent III	Weymann H30/26R	1948-49
RT1107-1151	JXN 135-179	AEC Regent III	Weymann H30/26R	1949
RT1152-1181	JXC 460-489	AEC Regent III	Saunders H30/26R	1948-49
RT1182-1251	KGK 651-720	AEC Regent III	Saunders H30/26R	1949
RT1252-1351	KLB 501-600	AEC Regent III	Saunders H30/26R	1949-50
RT1352-1401	KXW 451-500	AEC Regent III	Saunders H30/26R	1950
RT1402-1428	JXC 165-191	AEC Regent III	Cravens H30/26R	1948-49
RT1429-1461	JXC 192-224	AEC Regent III	Cravens H30/26R	1949
RT1462-1521	KGK 721-780	AEC Regent III	Cravens H30/26R	1949-50
RT1522-1529	KGU 236-243	AEC Regent III	Park Royal H30/26R	1949
RT1530-1540	KGU 290-300	AEC Regent III	Park Royal H30/26R	1949
RT1541-1547	KGU 410-416	AEC Regent III	Park Royal H30/26R	1949
RT1548-1558	KGU 440-450	AEC Regent III	Park Royal H30/26R	1949
RT1559-1566	KLB 631-638	AEC Regent III	Park Royal H30/26R	1949
RT1567-1590	KLB 655-678	AEC Regent III	Park Royal H30/26R	1949
RT1591-1628	KLB 713-750	AEC Regent III	Park Royal H30/26R	1950
RT1629-1654	KXW 251-276	AEC Regent III	Park Royal H30/26R	1950
RT1655-1697	KXW 301-343	AEC Regent III	Park Royal H30/26R	1950

- RT1 originally entered service in June 1938 as ST1140, fitted with a 1931 open-staircase Dodson body transferred from a Leyland Titan TD1. It re-entered service with its new RT-type body in June 1939.
- RT657 was to have been JXC 20; this registration was allocated to LT's first Leyland Titan PD2, RTL501.

For most of the 1950s the only double-deck coaches on Green Line service were 36 Weymann-bodied RTs delivered in 1950 which were followed by a further 21 in 1954 with Park Royal bodies transferred from SRTs. Travel-stained RT4508 at Aldgate in 1961 is a 1954 bus. Green Line buses did not carry exterior advertising. *Iain MacGregor*

RT1698-1730	KYY 525-557	AEC Regent III	Park Royal H30/26R	1950
RT1731-1794	KYY 569-632	AEC Regent III	Park Royal H30/26R	1950
RT1795-1849	KYY 650-704	AEC Regent III	Park Royal H30/26R	1950
RT1850-1854	KYY 716-720	AEC Regent III	Park Royal H30/26R	1950
RT1855-1885	LLU 741-771	AEC Regent III	Park Royal H30/26R	1950
RT1886-1910	LLU 794-818	AEC Regent III	Park Royal H30/26R	1950
RT1911-1920	LLU 831-840	AEC Regent III	Park Royal H30/26R	1950
RT1921-1942	LUC 1-22	AEC Regent III	Park Royal H30/26R	1950
RT1943-1954	LUC 29-40	AEC Regent III	Park Royal H30/26R	1950
RT1955-1978	LUC 44-67	AEC Regent III	Park Royal H30/26R	1950
RT1979-1999	LUC 80-100	AEC Regent III	Park Royal H30/26R	1950
RT2000-2023	LUC 226-249	AEC Regent III	Park Royal H30/26R	1950
RT2024-2039	LUC 266-281	AEC Regent III	Park Royal H30/26R	1950
RT2040-2056	LUC 288-304	AEC Regent III	Park Royal H30/26R	1950-51
RT2057-2062	LUC 320-325	AEC Regent III	Park Royal H30/26R	1951
RT2063-2095	LYF 1-33	AEC Regent III	Park Royal H30/26R	1951
RT2096-2112	LYF 72-88	AEC Regent III	Park Royal H30/26R	1951
RT2113-2115	LYF 168-170	AEC Regent III	Park Royal H30/26R	1951
RT2116	KLB 981	AEC Regent III	Weymann H30/26R	1949
RT2117-2121	KLB 982-986	AEC Regent III	Park Royal H30/26R	1949
RT2122-2171	KGK 931-980	AEC Regent III	Weymann H30/26R	1949
RT2172-2243	KGU 101-172	AEC Regent III	Weymann H30/26R	1949
RT2244-2270	KGU 173-199	AEC Regent III	Weymann H30/26R	1949
RT2271	KGU 200	AEC Regent III	Weymann H30/26R	1949
RT2272-2371	KGU 301-400	AEC Regent III	Weymann H30/26R	1949
RT2372-2471	KLB 751-850	AEC Regent III	Weymann H30/26R	1949-50

● RT2116-2121 were fitted when new with overhauled bodies from the body float at Aldenham.

The 120 Cravens-bodied RTs were immediately recognisable by their five-bay bodies. RT1402 was the first and was in Country Area green. It was new in 1948 and spent its seven-year life with LT in Watford.

RT2472-2498	KXW 101-127	AEC Regent III	Weymann H30/26R	1950
RT2499-2521	KXW 128-150	AEC Regent III	Weymann H30/26R	1950
RT2522-2551	LYF 171-200	AEC Regent III	Park Royal H30/26R	1951
RT2552-2651	LYF 277-376	AEC Regent III	Park Royal H30/26R	1951
RT2652-2774	LYR 636-758	AEC Regent III	Park Royal H30/26R	1951
RT2775-2776	LYR 826-827	AEC Regent III	Park Royal H30/26R	1952
RT2777-2791	LYR 941-955	AEC Regent III	Park Royal H30/26R	1952
RT2792-2829	LYR 962-999	AEC Regent III	Park Royal H30/26R	1952
RT2830-2853	LYF 477-500	AEC Regent III	Park Royal H30/26R	1952
RT2854-2865	MLL 501-512	AEC Regent III	Park Royal H30/26R	1952
RT2866-2928	MLL 613-675	AEC Regent III	Park Royal H30/26R	1952
RT2929-2937	MLL 688-696	AEC Regent III	Park Royal H30/26R	1952
RT2938-2946	MLL 704-712	AEC Regent III	Park Royal H30/26R	1952
RT2947	MXX 31	AEC Regent III	Park Royal H30/26R	1952
RT2948-2951	MXX 36-39	AEC Regent III	Park Royal H30/26R	1952
RT2952-2971	MXX 41-60	AEC Regent III	Park Royal H30/26R	1952
RT2972-2982	NLE 740-750	AEC Regent III	Park Royal H30/26R	1953
RT2983-3010	NLE 754-781	AEC Regent III	Park Royal H30/26R	1953
RT3011-3041	NLE 901-931	AEC Regent III	Park Royal H30/26R	1953
RT3042-3054	KXW 151-163	AEC Regent III	Weymann H30/26R	1950
RT3055-3114	KXW 164-223	AEC Regent III	Weymann H30/26R	1950
RT3115-3141	KXW 224-250	AEC Regent III	Weymann H30/26R	1950
RT3142-3241	KYY 871-970	AEC Regent III	Weymann H30/26R	1950
RT3242-3259	LLU 601-618	AEC Regent III	Weymann H30/26R	1950
RT3260-3281	LLU 619-640	AEC Regent III	Weymann H30/26R	1950
RT3282-3416	LYR 501-635	AEC Regent III	Weymann H30/26R	1951-52
RT3417-3463	LYR 836-882	AEC Regent III	Weymann H30/26R	1952

RT3464-3494	LYR 883-913	AEC Regent III	Weymann H30/26R	1952
RT3495-3515	LYR 914-934	AEC Regent III	Weymann H30/26R	1952
RT3516-3533	MLL 826-843	AEC Regent III	Weymann H30/26R	1952
RT3534-3596	MLL 844-906	AEC Regent III	Weymann H30/26R	1952
RT3597-3615	MLL 907-925	AEC Regent III	Weymann H30/26R	1952
RT3616-3636	MXX 131-151	AEC Regent III	Weymann H30/26R	1952
RT3637-3646	MXX 152-161	AEC Regent III	Weymann H30/26R	1952-53
RT3647-3683	MXX 162-198	AEC Regent III	Weymann H30/26R	1953
RT3684-3693	MXX 199-208	AEC Regent III	Weymann H30/26R	1953
RT3694-3718	NLE 801-825	AEC Regent III	Weymann H30/26R	1953
RT3719-3735	NLE 826-832	AEC Regent III	Weymann H30/26R	1953
RT3736-3793	NLE 833-900	AEC Regent III	Weymann H30/26R	1953
RT3794-3806	NXP 801-813	AEC Regent III	Weymann H30/26R	1953
RT3807-3816	NXP 814-823	AEC Regent III	Weymann H30/26R	1953
RT3817-3841	NXP 824-848	AEC Regent III	Weymann H30/26R	1953
RT3842-3856	LLU 641-655	AEC Regent III	Weymann H30/26R	1950
RT3857-3859	LLU 656-658	AEC Regent III	Weymann H30/26R	1950
RT3860-3899	LLU 659-698	AEC Regent III	Weymann H30/26R	1950
RT3900-3901	LLU 699-700	AEC Regent III	Weymann H30/26R	1950
RT3902-3941	LLU 701-740	AEC Regent III	Weymann H30/26R	1950
RT3942-4030	LUC 101-189	AEC Regent III	Weymann H30/26R	1950-51
RT4031-4041	LUC 190-200	AEC Regent III	Weymann H30/26R	1951
RT4042-4050	LUC 391-399	AEC Regent III	Weymann H30/26R	1951
RT4051-4098	LUC 400-447	AEC Regent III	Weymann H30/26R	1951
RT4099-4126	LUC 448-475	AEC Regent III	Weymann H30/26R	1951
RT4127-4141	LUC 476-490	AEC Regent III	Weymann H30/26R	1951
RT4142-4160	LYF 201-219	AEC Regent III	Weymann H30/26R	1951
RT4161-4207	LYF 220-266	AEC Regent III	Weymann H30/26R	1951
RT4208-4217	LYF 267-276	AEC Regent III	Weymann H30/26R	1951
RT4218-4267	KYY 821-870	AEC Regent III	Saunders H30/26R	1950-51
RT4268-4335	NLE 932-999	AEC Regent III	Park Royal H30/26R	1953
RT4336-4396	NLP 501-561	AEC Regent III	Park Royal H30/26R	1953
RT4397-4437	NXP 751-791	AEC Regent III	Park Royal H30/26R	1953
RT4438	NXP 792	AEC Regent III	Park Royal H30/26R	1953
RT4439-4446	NXP 793-800	AEC Regent III	Park Royal H30/26R	1953-54
RT4447-4472	OLD 667-692	AEC Regent III	Park Royal H30/26R	1954
RT4473	OLD 693	AEC Regent III	Park Royal H30/26R	1954
RT4474	OLD 694	AEC Regent III	Park Royal H30/26R	1954
RT4475-4480	OLD 695-700	AEC Regent III	Park Royal H30/26R	1954
RT4481-4482	OLD 701-702	AEC Regent III	Park Royal H30/26R	1954
RT4483-4484	OLD 703-704	AEC Regent III	Park Royal H30/26R	1954
RT4485-4486	OLD 705-706	AEC Regent III	Park Royal H30/26R	1954
RT4487-4556	OLD 707-776	AEC Regent III	Park Royal H30/26R	1954
RT4557-4568	NXP 849-860	AEC Regent III	Weymann H30/26R	1953
RT4569-4607	NLP 562-600	AEC Regent III	Park Royal H30/26R	1953
RT4608-4667	NXP 861-920	AEC Regent III	Park Royal H30/26R	1953-54
RT4668	MXX 40	AEC Regent III	Park Royal H30/26R	1953
RT4669-4684	NXP 921-936	AEC Regent III	Park Royal H30/26R	1954
RT4685-4714	NXP 970-999	AEC Regent III	Weymann H30/26R	1953-54
RT4715-4721	OLD 501-507	AEC Regent III	Weymann H30/26R	1954

● RT4397-4556 had bodies transferred from SRT chassis.

THE RT FAMILY

RT4722-4749	OLD 508-535	AEC Regent III	Weymann H30/26R	1954
RT4750-4759	OLD 537-546	AEC Regent III	Weymann H30/26R	1954
RT4760	OLD 547	AEC Regent III	Weymann H30/26R	1954
RT4761-4783	OLD 548-570	AEC Regent III	Weymann H30/26R	1954
RT4784-4793	OLD 821-830	AEC Regent III	Weymann H30/26R	1954
RT4794	OLD 861	AEC Regent III	Weymann H30/26R	1954
RT4795-4812	NXP 937-954	AEC Regent III	Park Royal H30/26R	1954
RT4813-4825	OLD 577-589	AEC Regent III	Park Royal H30/26R	1954

- RT4760 was to have been a green Country Area bus but was instead painted red for use at a trade fair in Holland, and retained that livery when it entered service with LT.
- RT4761 had a chassis built in 1947 which was fitted with a prewar Tilling body and used as a training unit operating on trade plates. It was first registered in 1954 when its new Weymann body was fitted.
- Country Area buses RT4727-4759, 4761-4794 were stored when new and entered service between 1956 and 1959.

RTC AEC Regent

| RTC1 | FXT 272 | AEC Regent | LPTB H26/20RD | 1940 |

- RTC1 was a Green Line coach based on an extensive rebuild of RT97 at Chiswick Works in 1949.

RTL Leyland Titan PD2 7RT

RTL1-12	JXN 313-324	Leyland Titan PD2	Park Royal H30/26R	1948
RTL13-22	JXN 333-342	Leyland Titan PD2	Park Royal H30/26R	1948
RTL23	JXN 344	Leyland Titan PD2	Park Royal H30/26R	1948
RTL24-116	JXN 347-439	Leyland Titan PD2	Park Royal H30/26R	1948-49
RTL117-252	KGK 781-916	Leyland Titan PD2	Park Royal H30/26R	1949
RTL253-254	KGK 929-930	Leyland Titan PD2	Park Royal H30/26R	1949
RTL255-285	KGU 201-231	Leyland Titan PD2	Park Royal H30/26R	1949
RTL286-331	KGU 244-289	Leyland Titan PD2	Park Royal H30/26R	1949
RTL332-340	KGU 401-409	Leyland Titan PD2	Park Royal H30/26R	1949
RTL341-363	KGU 417-439	Leyland Titan PD2	Park Royal H30/26R	1949
RTL364-413	KGU 451-500	Leyland Titan PD2	Park Royal H30/26R	1949

A remarkable 1949 rebuild transformed RT97 into striking 46-seat Green Line coach RTC1. It spent less than a year on Green Line service before being demoted to Country Area bus operation. *LT*

THE RT FAMILY

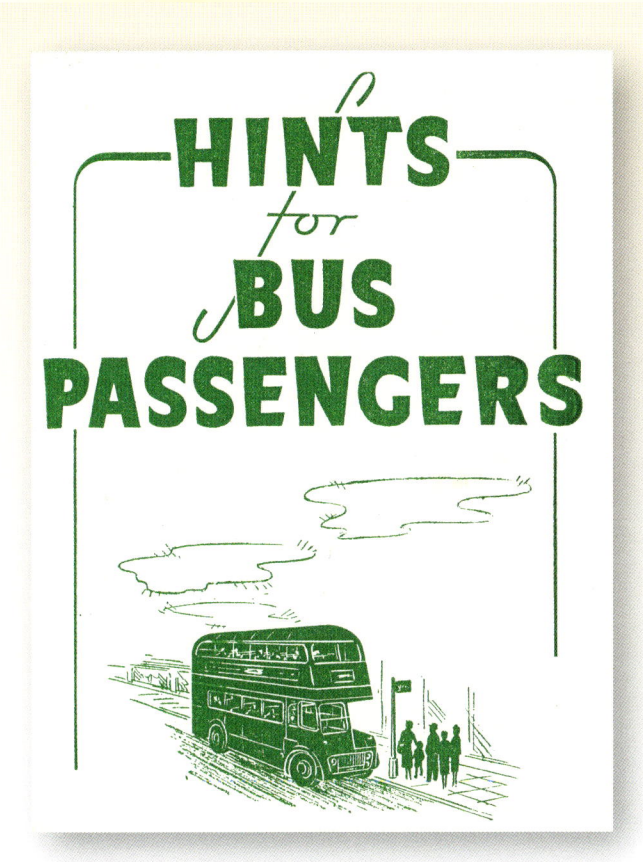

The Royal Society for the Prevention of Accidents wanted to illustrate a modern bus on a little safety leaflet in 1949. And what could have been more modern than RTC1?

RTL414-443	KLB 601-630	Leyland Titan PD2	Park Royal H30/26R	1949
RTL444-459	KLB 639-654	Leyland Titan PD2	Park Royal H30/26R	1949
RTL460-492	KLB 679-711	Leyland Titan PD2	Park Royal H30/26R	1950
RTL493-500	KXW 277-284	Leyland Titan PD2	Park Royal H30/26R	1950
RTL501	JXC 20	Leyland Titan PD2	Park Royal H30/26R	1948
RTL502-517	KXW 285-300	Leyland Titan PD2	Park Royal H30/26R	1950
RTL518-524	KXW 344-350	Leyland Titan PD2	Park Royal H30/26R	1950
RTL525-528	KYY 521-524	Leyland Titan PD2	Park Royal H30/26R	1950
RTL529-539	KYY 558-568	Leyland Titan PD2	Park Royal H30/26R	1950
RTL540-550	KYY 633-643	Leyland Titan PD2	Park Royal H30/26R	1950
RTL551-650	KGU 1-100	Leyland Titan PD2	Metro-Cammell H30/26R	1949-50
RTL651-750	KXW 1-100	Leyland Titan PD2	Metro-Cammell H30/26R	1950
RTL751-850	KYY 721-820	Leyland Titan PD2	Metro-Cammell H30/26R	1950
RTL851-950	LLU841-940	Leyland Titan PD2	Metro-Cammell H30/26R	1950
RTL951-1000	LUC 326-375	Leyland Titan PD2	Metro-Cammell H30/26R	1950-51
RTL1001-1006	KYY 644-649	Leyland Titan PD2	Park Royal H30/26R	1950
RTL1007-1017	KYY 705-715	Leyland Titan PD2	Park Royal H30/26R	1950
RTL1018-1039	LLU 772-793	Leyland Titan PD2	Park Royal H30/26R	1950
RTL1040-1051	LLU 819-830	Leyland Titan PD2	Park Royal H30/26R	1950
RTL1052-1057	LUC 23-28	Leyland Titan PD2	Park Royal H30/26R	1950
RTL1058-1060	LUC 41-43	Leyland Titan PD2	Park Royal H30/26R	1950
RTL1061-1072	LUC 68-79	Leyland Titan PD2	Park Royal H30/26R	1950
RTL1073-1088	LUC 250-265	Leyland Titan PD2	Park Royal H30/26R	1950
RTL1089-1094	LUC 282-287	Leyland Titan PD2	Park Royal H30/26R	1950

- RTL501 was the first RTL, delivered at the start of 1948. It was numbered after the 500 8ft-wide Titans on order which were going to be RTL1-500 but when delivered formed a new RTW class.

Park Royal-bodied RTL1313 of 1952 in Duncannon Street, with St Martin-in-the-Fields church hidden by scaffolding, is followed by 8ft-wide RTW36. The RTL has the standard postwar destination display while the RTW has a reduced display, a temporary expedient to conserve material in the late 1940s. The billboards on the right promote two now defunct newspapers, the *Sunday Dispatch* and the *News of the World*.

RTL1095-1109	LUC 305-319	Leyland Titan PD2	Park Royal H30/26R	1951
RTL1110-1147	LYF 34-71	Leyland Titan PD2	Park Royal H30/26R	1951
RTL1148-1226	LYF 89-167	Leyland Titan PD2	Park Royal H30/26R	1951
RTL1227-1293	LYR 759-825	Leyland Titan PD2	Park Royal H30/26R	1951-52
RTL1294-1301	LYR 828-835	Leyland Titan PD2	Park Royal H30/26R	1952
RTL1302-1306	LYR 936-940	Leyland Titan PD2	Park Royal H30/26R	1952
RTL1307	LYR 935	Leyland Titan PD2	Weymann H30/26R	1952
RTL1308-1313	LYR 956-961	Leyland Titan PD2	Park Royal H30/26R	1952
RTL1314-1325	MLL 676-687	Leyland Titan PD2	Park Royal H30/26R	1952
RTL1326-1332	MLL 697-703	Leyland Titan PD2	Park Royal H30/26R	1952
RTL1333-1336	MXX32-35	Leyland Titan PD2	Park Royal H30/26R	1952
RTL1337	OLD 813	Leyland Titan PD2	Park Royal H30/26R	1952
RTL1338-1407	MXX 61-130	Leyland Titan PD2	Park Royal H30/26R	1952-53
RTL1408-1413	MXX 215-220	Leyland Titan PD2	Park Royal H30/26R	1953
RTL1414-1426	NLE 501-513	Leyland Titan PD2	Park Royal H30/26R	1953
RTL1427-1465	NLE 701-739	Leyland Titan PD2	Park Royal H30/26R	1953
RTL1466-1468	NLE 751-753	Leyland Titan PD2	Park Royal H30/26R	1953
RTL1469-1474	NXP 955-960	Leyland Titan PD2	Park Royal H30/26R	1954

RTL1475-1480	OLD 571-576	Leyland Titan PD2	Park Royal H30/26R	1954
RTL1481-1557	OLD 590-666	Leyland Titan PD2	Park Royal H30/26R	1954
RTL1558-1593	OLD 777-812	Leyland Titan PD2	Park Royal H30/26R	1954
RTL1594-1600	OLD 814-820	Leyland Titan PD2	Park Royal H30/26R	1954
RTL1601	OLD 536	Leyland Titan PD2	Weymann H30/26R	1954
RTL1602-1631	OLD 831-860	Leyland Titan PD2	Weymann H30/26R	1954

- Out-of-sequence Weymann-bodied RTL1307 was used when new on a promotional tour of the USA and Canada.
- RTL1337 was used for tests at the Motor Industry Research Association and was not licensed until 1954.
- RTL1568-1600, 1602-1631 were stored when new and did not enter service until 1958.

RTW Leyland Titan PD2 6RT

RTW1-150	KGK 501-650	Leyland Titan PD2	Leyland H30/26R	1949
RTW151-250	KLB 881-980	Leyland Titan PD2	Leyland H30/26R	1949-50
RTW251-350	KXW 351-450	Leyland Titan PD2	Leyland H30/26R	1950
RTW351-450	LLU 501-600	Leyland Titan PD2	Leyland H30/26R	1950
RTW451-500	LLU 941-990	Leyland Titan PD2	Leyland H30/26R	1950

- These were originally intended to be numbered RTL1-500.

It says something about the importance of London Transport's orders to bus manufacturers that Leyland chose to feature a ten-year-old RTL in a 1961 *Bus & Coach* advert, rather than a more modern Titan with a new-look front, or even an Atlantean, both types of which are shown in the small illustrations on the left. Leyland had bought the Standard Triumph business in 1960, hence the relatively unusual Standard Vanguard Vignale on the right of the illustration.

ABOVE: RTW130 at Clapham Common on route 45 illustrates the slightly squatter appearance of these 8ft-wide buses when compared with standard RTs and RTLs. All 500 RTWs were bodied by Leyland. The 45 was a circuitous hour-long route which started north of the Thames at Farringdon Street, headed south over Blackfriars Bridge then passed through Brixton, Stockwell and Clapham before recrossing the river by Battersea Bridge to terminate at South Kensington. *Iain MacGregor*

LEFT: As a measure of stability new double-deck buses are required to be tilt tested to an angle of 28 degrees from the vertical before they can be certified for operation. RTW1 passes the test on the tilt table at Leyland. Guy ropes are in place to secure the bus if it starts to tip over. *Leyland*

SRT AEC Regent

The SRT class comprised 160 prewar STL-class AEC Regent chassis with 7.7-litre engines. They were rebuilt in 1949 to resemble the standard RT, complete with lowered radiator and bonnet, and fitted with new Park Royal bodies to the standard RT design. The chassis were new in 1937 (DGX, DLU, DYL, EGO), 1938 (ELP) or 1939 (FJJ, FXT). The bodies on the 160 SRTs were fitted to new AEC Regent IIIs RT4397-4556 in 1953-54.

Only the 1937 registration number identifies SRT154, seen here at Canons Park, as a rebuild of a prewar Regent rather than a genuine new Regent III. There were 160 SRTs, all bodied by Park Royal in 1949. The bold advert on the side simply reads "Selfridges" with no need for any explanation by London's second-biggest department store.

SRT1	FJJ 746	SRT9	FXT 60	SRT17	FXT 63	SRT25	FJJ 691
SRT2	FJJ 680	SRT10	FJJ 721	SRT18	FJJ 716	SRT26	FXT 67
SRT3	FJJ 690	SRT11	FJJ 717	SRT19	FXT 62	SRT27	FJJ 692
SRT4	FXT 53	SRT12	FJJ 725	SRT20	FXT 64	SRT28	FXT 75
SRT5	FJJ 756	SRT13	FJJ 754	SRT21	FXT 68	SRT29	FJJ 736
SRT6	FJJ 700	SRT14	FJJ 686	SRT22	FJJ 737	SRT30	FXT 83
SRT7	FJJ 676	SRT15	FJJ 707	SRT23	FJJ 769	SRT31	FXT 87
SRT8	FXT 56	SRT16	FJJ 750	SRT24	FXT 61	SRT32	FXT 57

SRT33	FXT 70	SRT66	FJJ 697	SRT99	FJJ 719	SRT132	DLU 93
SRT34	FJJ 696	SRT67	FXT 94	SRT100	FJJ 739	SRT133	DLU 102
SRT35	FJJ 684	SRT68	FJJ 687	SRT101	FJJ 677	SRT134	DLU 67
SRT36	FJJ 688	SRT69	FJJ 733	SRT102	FJJ 713	SRT135	EGO 395
SRT37	FXT 72	SRT70	FJJ 732	SRT103	FJJ 758	SRT136	EGO 342
SRT38	FXT 73	SRT71	FJJ 712	SRT104	FJJ 715	SRT137	DYL 812
SRT39	FJJ 759	SRT72	FJJ 730	SRT105	FJJ 708	SRT138	EGO 463
SRT40	FJJ 747	SRT73	FXT 81	SRT106	FXT 86	SRT139	DLU 100
SRT41	FXT 88	SRT74	FJJ 678	SRT107	FJJ 706	SRT140	EGO 466
SRT42	FXT 49	SRT75	FJJ 699	SRT108	FJJ 704	SRT141	EGO 488
SRT43	FXT 80	SRT76	FJJ 735	SRT109	FJJ 693	SRT142	DLU 101
SRT44	FJJ 752	SRT77	FJJ 718	SRT110	FJJ 742	SRT143	ELP 171
SRT45	FJJ 711	SRT78	FJJ 734	SRT111	FJJ 710	SRT144	DLU 60
SRT46	FJJ 731	SRT79	FXT 66	SRT112	FJJ 740	SRT145	DLU 118
SRT47	FXT 77	SRT80	FJJ 748	SRT113	FJJ 749	SRT146	DLU 84
SRT48	FJJ 705	SRT81	FXT 52	SRT114	FJJ 714	SRT147	DLU 24
SRT49	FJJ 751	SRT82	FXT 90	SRT115	FJJ 724	SRT148	ELP 126
SRT50	FXT 65	SRT83	FXT 95	SRT116	FJJ 701	SRT149	DLU 129
SRT51	FXT 89	SRT84	FJJ 682	SRT117	FJJ 741	SRT150	EGO 407
SRT52	FXT 58	SRT85	FXT 50	SRT118	FJJ 702	SRT151	EGO 459
SRT53	FXT 54	SRT86	FJJ 757	SRT119	FJJ 694	SRT152	DLU 25
SRT54	FJJ 753	SRT87	FJJ 709	SRT120	FXT 82	SRT153	DLU 96
SRT55	FXT 76	SRT88	FXT 79	SRT121	FJJ 743	SRT154	DLU 54
SRT56	FJJ 683	SRT89	FXT 51	SRT122	FJJ 745	SRT155	DLU 74
SRT57	FXT 93	SRT90	FJJ 727	SRT123	FJJ 728	SRT156	DYL 857
SRT58	FXT 92	SRT91	FJJ 681	SRT124	FJJ 689	SRT157	DYL 807
SRT59	FJJ 695	SRT92	FXT 59	SRT125	FXT 91	SRT158	DLU 110
SRT60	FXT 71	SRT93	FJJ 726	SRT126	DLU 126	SRT159	EGO 453
SRT61	FXT 85	SRT94	FJJ 720	SRT127	DLU 56	SRT160	EGO 482
SRT62	FXT 74	SRT95	FXT 78	SRT128	DLU 103		
SRT63	FJJ 723	SRT96	FJJ 698	SRT129	DYL 819		
SRT64	FXT 84	SRT97	FJJ 738	SRT130	DLU 86		
SRT65	FXT 55	SRT98	FJJ 729	SRT131	DGX 352		

AEC Regal IV

London Transport bought 211 half-cab Leyland Tigers and AEC Regals between 1946 and 1948, and in 1951-52 followed these with the new-generation underfloor-engined AEC Regal IV, building up a fleet of 700 RF models and 15 of the more luxurious RFW. They were powered by a horizontal version of the 9.6-litre engine fitted to the RT-class AEC Regents and like the RTs had a four-speed preselector gearbox. While these were London's first postwar buses to adopt what at the time was a novel engine layout, it's worth remembering that LT had tried unconventional types of single-deckers in the 1930s with the side-engined AEC Q of which there were 234 plus four double-deckers, the 88 TF-class underfloor-engined Leyland Tigers and the 49-strong CR-class of rear-engined Leyland Cubs.

When AEC was developing the Regal IV the maximum length for a two-axle single-deck bus was 27ft 6in and the first 25 RFs were built to this length. They were 35-seat private-hire

The majority of the RF class AECs were supplied in green rather than red, and included 263 Green Line coaches. RF62 is at Englefield Green, Surrey, on its way from Windsor to Harlow in 1962. Martin Llewellyn/Omnicolour

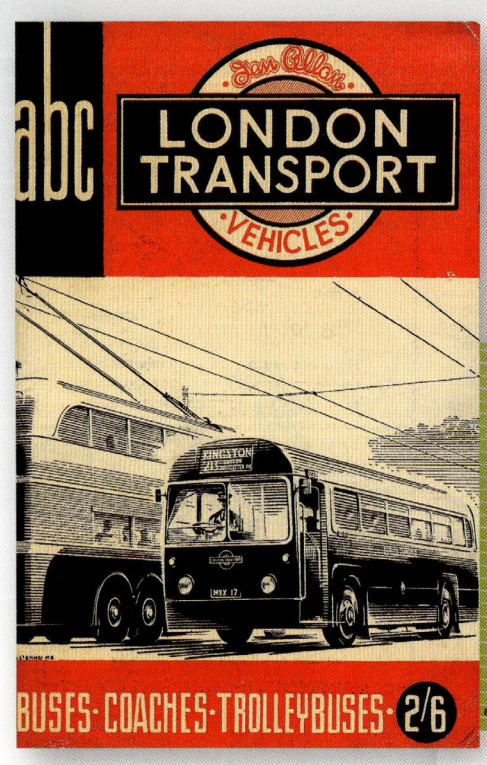

BELOW: The bodies which Metro-Cammell built for the RFs were of a design supplied exclusively to LT. Perhaps it was the prestige attached to the 700-vehicle order which saw MCW produce a dedicated RF brochure in 1954.

ABOVE: A scraper-board drawing of AEC Regal IV RF375 by A N Wolstenholme appeared on the cover of the 1953 edition of the Ian Allan *ABC of London Transport Vehicles*. Wolstenholme provided the illustrations for most of the covers of Ian Allan's ABC books in the 1950s. *Gavin Booth collection*

coaches in a green and grey livery with glazed cove panels featuring Triplex toughened glass. They were followed by 263 Green Line coaches with 39 seats in a Metro-Cammell body built to the revised maximum length of 30ft, which had been authorised in 1950. The remaining RFs were 30ft-long 41-seat buses, with 225 for Central Area services and 187 for the Country Area. As with front-entrance single-deckers elsewhere in Britain the Country Area RFs had doors on the entrance; those for the Central Area did not. Unusually for underfloor-engined buses in Britain the RFs were built to a width of 7ft 6in rather than 8ft.

The surviving Country Area and Green Line RFs passed to London Country in 1971. The last of the red RFs were withdrawn by LT in 1979.

The RFWs were 8ft wide and had unusual and attractive ECW bodies of a style supplied only to LT and to Tillings Travel of London, which had five. Like the private hire RFs, the RFWs were painted green and grey. All 15 were sold in 1964, with ten being exported to Ceylon.

LT also operated 65 Regal IVs on behalf of BEA (see page 52).

Specifications

Model	Engine	Displacement	Power output	Gearbox
AEC Regal IV	AEC A219	9.6 litres	125bhp	AEC four-speed preselector

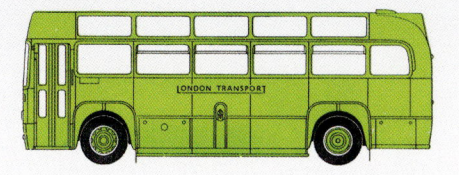

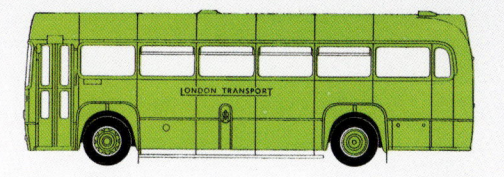

These drawings from MCW's brochure illustrate the difference in length between the first 25 RFs (left) and the main fleet which followed.

RF1-25	LUC 201-225	AEC Regal IV 9821LT	Metro-Cammell B35F	1951
RF26-125	LYF 377-476	AEC Regal IV 9821LT	Metro-Cammell B39F	1951-52
RF126-225	MLL 513-612	AEC Regal IV 9821LT	Metro-Cammell B39F	1952
RF226-288	MLL 763-825	AEC Regal IV 9821LT	Metro-Cammell B39F	1952
RF289-358	MLL 926-995	AEC Regal IV 9821LT	Metro-Cammell B41F	1952
RF359-388	MXX 1-30	AEC Regal IV 9821LT	Metro-Cammell B41F	1952
RF389-411	MXX 277-299	AEC Regal IV 9821LT	Metro-Cammell B41F	1952
RF412-513	MXX 389-490	AEC Regal IV 9821LT	Metro-Cammell B41F	1952-53
RF514-700	NLE 514-700	AEC Regal IV 9821LT	Metro-Cammell B41F	1953

- RF1-25 were private hire coaches.
- RF26-288 were Green Line coaches.
- RF514-700 were Country Area buses.

| RFW1-15 | LUC 376-390 | AEC Regal IV 9821E | ECW C39F | 1951 |

- RFW1-15 were private hire coaches.

The RFW class of AEC Regal IVs had proper coach bodies by ECW with glazed cove panels, 39 high-backed seats and a single-piece hinged door. RFW8 unloads at Heathrow Airport in 1957. This green and grey livery was also used on the 25 RF coaches. *Geoffrey Morant*

BEA coaches

In 1952 London Transport took over operation of the coach services which carried British European Airways passengers from BEA's central London terminal to Northolt and Heathrow airports. The services had previously been operated by BEA using ex-British Overseas Airways Corporation Commer Commando coaches. These had petrol engines and 20-seat Park Royal bodies. The new vehicles were owned by BEA but maintained and largely specified by LT. The first generation of coaches used the 8ft-wide version of the AEC Regal IV chassis fitted with what were generally described as half-deck coach bodies, similar to those on the Commers they were replacing. They were 37-seaters with 21 of the seats in the raised area at the rear over the capacious luggage boot.

Half-deck coaches were never common. The key feature of the design was plenty of room for luggage in the space below the raised rear section. The AEC Regal IVs which LT operated for BEA had 37-seat Park Royal bodies with a centre entrance. Brand new MLL 755 heads along Piccadilly in the summer of 1953 to connect with an SAS flight to Oslo.

BEA's Regal IVs were replaced by forward-entrance Routemasters in 1966-67. When new they carried this livery. *Chris Drew*

Eight AEC Reliances with AH590 engines and Willowbrook coach bodies operated the BEA Executive Express between central London and Heathrow Airport. EC2 is at the airline's terminal in Gloucester Road. *GVVT archive*

In 1961 a solitary AEC Regent V double-decker was evaluated as a potential replacement for the Regal IVs. This had a large luggage locker at the rear of the lower saloon, and seated only 55 passengers rather than the 72 of a typical 30ft-long double-decker of the time. The Regent had a 128bhp AV590 engine and AEC's Monocontrol transmission.

The second generation BEA fleet was delivered in 1966-67, when 65 forward-entrance Routemasters replaced the 14-year-old half-decks. This followed a trial in 1964 of the original forward-entrance Routemaster, RMF1254, which addressed the challenge of accommodating air travellers' luggage by towing a two-wheel trailer. The BEA Routemasters had luggage trailers and carried 56 passengers compared with 37 on the vehicles they were replacing. To give a high top speed on the M4 motorway they had 175bhp AV690 engines and a high-ratio rear axle. Other features were twin headlights and rear air suspension, features carried over from the Green Line Routemaster coaches.

The Routemasters ran in two different BEA liveries then, from 1974, in British Airways colours following the amalgamation of BEA and BOAC. The service ended in March 1979, rendered superfluous by the opening of the Piccadilly Line extension to Heathrow Airport.

EC1-8 were 36ft-long AEC Reliances for a new Executive Express service which operated from central London and provided business travellers with an airside connection at Heathrow in those happy days when airport security was more relaxed than it is now. To allow their operation on the tarmac at Heathrow they had a flashing orange beacon on the roof. The Reliances had 153bhp AH590 engines and ZF six-speed synchromesh gearboxes and bodies by Willowbrook of Loughborough. They were fitted with radio telephones for passengers' use. When it was introduced in 1966 the premium service carried a premium fare of 10 shillings (50p) compared with 5 shillings (25p) for the standard service operated by the half-deck Regal IVs.

	MLL 713-762	AEC Regal IV 9822E	Park Royal HDC37C	1952-53
	NLP 636-650	AEC Regal IV 9822E	Park Royal HDC37C	1953
	220 CXK	AEC Regent V 2D2RA	Park Royal H38/17F	1961

● This bus received the last registration in a batch of 40 numbers (181-220 CXK) booked for service vehicles.

	KGJ 601-625D	AEC Routemaster R2RH	Park Royal H32/24F	1966
	NMY 626-665E	AEC Routemaster R2RH	Park Royal H32/24F	1967
EC1-8	KHM 1-8D	AEC Reliance 2U3RA	Willowbrook C49F	1966

AEC Routemaster

Is the Routemaster Britain's most famous bus? Probably. The Routemaster was technically advanced when it was being developed by London Transport in the mid 1950s. Its aluminium structure was strong, light and – as time would show – durable, with some buses lasting in regular service in London until 2005, by which time they were 45 years old. Most urban buses start heading for the scrapyard after 15 years or less. The Routemaster did not have a conventional chassis, but was instead of integral construction with front and rear subframes. In this it was ahead of its time. It also had coil spring suspension and hydraulic brakes.

RM2 had its radiator located at the front, unlike RM1 on which it was behind the engine under the saloon floor. The new layout was made possible by a relaxation in the length limit for two-axle double-deckers. It operated as a Country Area green bus for a few months in the summer of 1957, running on the 406, Reigate to Kingston. Here it is posed on Epsom Downs. *LT*

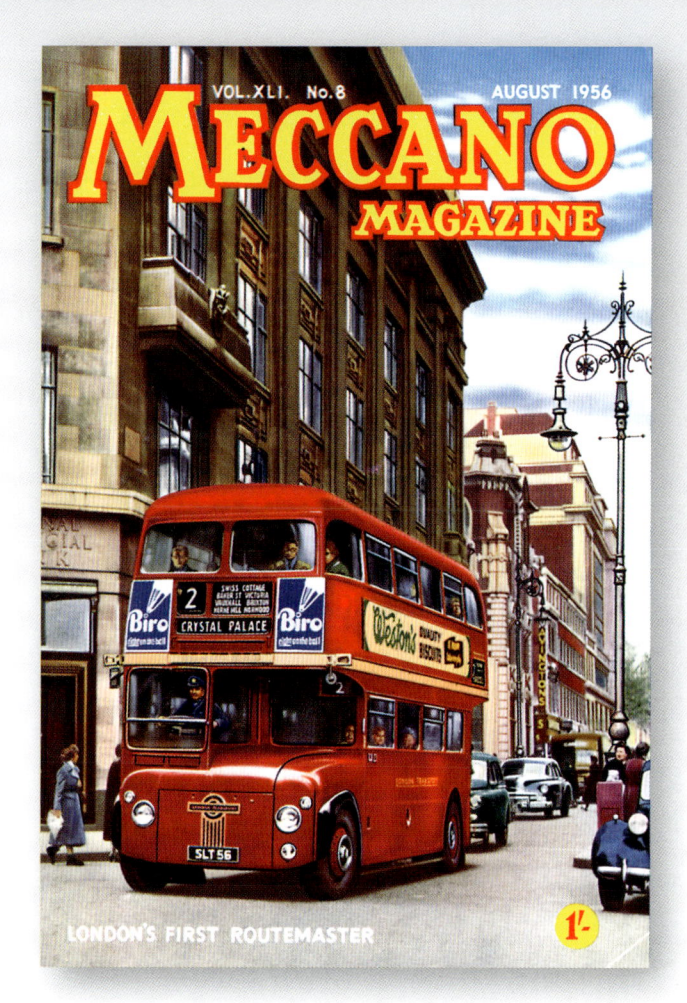

Although it was completed in 1954, prototype Routemaster RM1 did not enter service until January 1956. In August of that year it appeared on the cover of *Meccano Magazine*, a popular monthly aimed at boys buying Meccano products which included Hornby Trains and Dinky Toys. The magazine cost one shilling (5p). The coloured illustration is based on a black-and-white photograph taken at the junction of Baker Street and Marylebone Road.

Four prototypes were built between 1954 and 1957, and an order for 850 buses was announced by LT in September 1956, at which point the first prototype, RM1, had been in service for just six months.

The standard Routemaster R2RH (**R**outemaster, **2**-pedal control, **R**ight-hand drive, **H**ydraulic brakes) was 27ft 6in long and was powered by an AEC AV590 engine. Between 1961 and 1964 Leyland O.600 engines were fitted to 576 buses, classed as 2R2RH. Apart from the four prototypes, all of the Routemasters were built by Park Royal. The standard buses were 64-seaters and weighed just 7tons 5cwt, which was half a ton lighter than a 56-seat RT.

A new generation of double-deck Green Line coaches in the shape of 68 Routemasters was delivered in 1962. These had 57 seats, platform doors, luggage racks, fluorescent lighting, 41 gallon fuel tanks (the standard was 29 gallons), twin headlights, air suspension instead of coil springs on the rear axle, and a revised rear axle ratio to give a higher maximum speed. The coaches also had semi-automatic rather than fully-automatic gearboxes. The logic for this was that the average number of gear changes per mile was four on a Green Line coach, compared with 15 on a Central Area bus.

A trial batch of two dozen 30ft-long versions of the Routemaster was evaluated in 1961. Changes to the structure were minimised by inserting a short bay in mid wheelbase. While this idea is generally associated with the long Routemasters it had in fact first been seen in the UK in 1958 on 30ft-long Northern Counties bodies on Leyland Titan PD3 chassis for Southdown Motor Services. The long Routemasters carried 72 passengers and weighed 7tons 15cwt; from 1965 all Routemasters for LT were built as 30ft-long 72-seaters. These included

100 for the Country Area in the winter of 1965-66 with semi-automatic rather than fully-automatic gearboxes. There were 30ft-long Green Line coach versions too. These had 65 seats and more powerful 11.3-litre AEC AV690 engines. The last were taken off Green Line service in 1976, bringing a temporary halt to double-deck Green Line operation.

Illuminated exterior advertising panels were briefly popular in the early 1960s. They were back-lit by fluorescent tubes and were normally located on the offside upper-deck side panels. They were fitted to 300 Central Area Routemasters.

There was also a solitary forward-entrance 30ft-long Routemaster, RMF1254, which never ran in service with LT. Fifty similar buses were built for Northern General Transport and the same layout was adopted for 65 short Routemasters used on BEA services from 1966, ordered after trials of RMF1254 by BEA.

The final development was a rear-engined version, FRM1, which appeared in 1966 but did not make it to series production. LT was temporarily enamoured with high-capacity single-deckers and Leyland (which had taken over AEC and Park Royal in 1962) saw no future for a complex and expensive competitor for its esisting rear-engined Atlantean. FRM1 was 31ft 3in long and had a transverse AV691 engine. It had fixed windows and a thermostatically-controlled Clayton Compass heating and ventilating system but shortly after entering service from Tottenham garage in June 1967 it was fitted with standard Routemaster quarter-drop opening windows. It later operated from Croydon and Potters Bar garages, and then from 1978 until withdrawal in 1983 it was used on the Round London Sightseeing Tour.

When London Country was formed in 1970 its fleet included 209 Routemasters, a mixture of Green Line coaches and green-liveried buses. At the end of the 1970s all but one (prototype RMC4) were bought back by LT and around half of them were refurbished for further service.

In most parts of Britain half-cab front-engined buses had disappeared by the start of the 1980s. But not in London. Problems with Daimler Fleetlines saw Routemasters being overhauled and extensively rebuilt. And those that were being withdrawn found willing buyers in the late 1980s when withdrawal was well under way, and many operators in deregulated Britain saw in the Routemaster a low-cost way of trying to fight off competition from new entrants to the bus business. The biggest buyer was the Scottish Bus Group with 168, most of which ran in Glasgow. Other notable users included Blackpool Transport, Burnley & Pendle, Cumberland Motor Services, East Yorkshire Motor Services, Greater Manchester Buses, Magicbus (Glasgow), Reading Mainline, Southampton Citybus, Southend Transport and United Counties.

And in London they soldiered on. Most of those which survived in 1990 had their original engines replaced by new units from Cummins and Iveco. Regular operation of Routemasters on a normal scheduled service in London finally ended in December 2005. The last route was the 159, Marble Arch to Streatham Station, operated by Arriva London South from Brixton garage, where the Routemasters were replaced by low-floor Volvo B7TLs.

Routemaster specifications

Model	Engine	Displacement	Power output	Gearbox
R2RH RM, RMC, RML	AEC AV590	9.6 litres	115bhp	AEC four-speed automatic
2R2RH RM	Leyland O.600	9.8 litres	115bhp	AEC four-speed automatic
R2RH RCL	AEC AV690	11.3 litres	150bhp	AEC four-speed automatic
R2RH BEA	AEC AV690	11.3 litres	175bhp	AEC four-speed automatic
FR2R FRM1	AEC AV691	11.3 litres	150bhp	AEC four-speed automatic

RM787 of 1961 enters Piccadilly Circus from Shaftesbury Avenue in 1979. The solid white roundel on the side was introduced in 1974.

The last 543 Routemasters, built between 1965 and 1968, were 30ft long and featured a short bay in the wheelbase which minimised the changes needed to create the lengthened body structure. There were 143 long Routemasters in green livery, 43 Green Line coaches and 100 Country Area buses which included RML2348 photographed at Bromley North in the company of a Central Area RT. *Geoffrey Morant*

RM1	SLT 56	AEC Routemaster	LTE H36/28R	1954
RM2	SLT 57	AEC Routemaster	LTE H36/28R	1955
RML3	SLT 58	AEC Routemaster	Weymann H36/28R	1957
CRL4	SLT 59	AEC Routemaster	ECW H32/25RD	1957
RM5-300	VLT 5-300	AEC Routemaster R2RH	Park Royal H36/28R	1959-60
RM301-631	WLT 301-631	AEC Routemaster R2RH	Park Royal H36/28R	1960-61
RM632	WLT 632	AEC Routemaster 2R2RH	Park Royal H36/28R	1961
RM633-869	WLT 633-869	AEC Routemaster R2RH	Park Royal H36/28R	1961
RM870	WLT 870	AEC Routemaster 2R2RH	Park Royal H36/28R	1961
RM871-879	WLT 871-879	AEC Routemaster R2RH	Park Royal H36/28R	1961

RML880-903	WLT 880-903	AEC Routemaster R2RH	Park Royal H40/32R	1961-62
RM904-999	WLT 904-999	AEC Routemaster R2RH	Park Royal H36/28R	1961
RM1000	100 BXL	AEC Routemaster R2RH	Park Royal H36/28R	1961
RM1001-1008	1-8 CLT	AEC Routemaster R2RH	Park Royal H36/28R	1961
RM1009	9 CLT	AEC Routemaster 2R2RH	Park Royal H36/28R	1961
RM1010-1253	10-253 CLT	AEC Routemaster R2RH	Park Royal H36/28R	1961-62
RMF1254	254 CLT	AEC Routemaster 3R2RH	Park Royal H38/31F	1962
RM1255-1452	255-452 CLT	AEC Routemaster 2R2RH	Park Royal H36/28R	1962-63
RMC1453-1520	453-520 CLT	AEC Routemaster R2RH	Park Royal H32/25RD	1962
RM1521-1600	521-600 CLT	AEC Routemaster 2R2RH	Park Royal H36/28R	1963
RM1601-1719	601-719 DYE	AEC Routemaster 2R2RH	Park Royal H36/28R	1963
RM1720-1810	720-810 DYE	AEC Routemaster R2RH	Park Royal H36/28R	1963-64
RM1811-1865	811-865DYE	AEC Routemaster 2R2RH	Park Royal H36/28R	1964
RM1866-1985	ALD 866-985B	AEC Routemaster 2R2RH	Park Royal H36/28R	1964
RM1986-1999	ALD 986-999B	AEC Routemaster R2RH	Park Royal H36/28R	1964
RM2000	ALM 200B	AEC Routemaster R2RH	Park Royal H36/28R	1964
RM2001-2105	ALM 1-105B	AEC Routemaster R2RH	Park Royal H36/28R	1964
RM2106-2217	CUV 106-217C	AEC Routemaster R2RH	Park Royal H36/28R	1965
RCL2218-2260	CUV 218-260C	AEC Routemaster R2RH	Park Royal H36/29RD	1965
RML2261-2305	CUV 261-305C	AEC Routemaster R2RH	Park Royal H40/32R	1965
RML2306-2355	CUV 306-355C	AEC Routemaster R2RH	Park Royal H40/32R	1965
RML2356-2363	CUV 356-363C	AEC Routemaster R2RH	Park Royal H40/32R	1965
RML2364-2410	JJD 364-410D	AEC Routemaster R2RH	Park Royal H40/32R	1966
RML2411-2460	JJD 411-460D	AEC Routemaster R2RH	Park Royal H40/32R	1966
RML2461-2598	JJD 461-598D	AEC Routemaster R2RH	Park Royal H40/32R	1966
RML2599-2657	NML 599-657E	AEC Routemaster R2RH	Park Royal H40/32R	1967
RML2658-2760	SMK 658-760F	AEC Routemaster R2RH	Park Royal H40/32R	1967-68

- RM1,2 were originally allocated registrations OLD 862/3.
- The 'L' in RML3 and CRL4 indicated a Leyland engine; they were later renumbered RM3, RMC4.
- RM2, RML2306-2355, 2411-2460 were originally green Country Area buses. All except RM2, RML2321, 2441/3 were transferred to London Country in 1970.
- CRL4, RMC1453-1520, RCL2218-2260 were Green Line coaches. All were transferred to London Country in 1970.
- RML880-903 were to have been numbered ER880-903.
- RMF1254 was not used in service by London Transport.
- RMC1453-1520 were to have been numbered CR1453-1520.

Rear-engined Routemaster prototype

FRM1	KGY 4D	AEC Routemaster FR2R	Park Royal H41/31F	1966

BEA Routemasters

	KGJ 601-625D	AEC Routemaster R2RH	Park Royal H32/24F	1966
	NMY 626-665E	AEC Routemaster R2RH	Park Royal H32/24F	1967

Former Northern General Routemasters purchased by LT in 1979-80

RMF2761	FPT 582C	AEC Routemaster 3R2RH	Park Royal H41/31F	1965
RMF2762-2763	FPT 584-585C	AEC Routemaster 3R2RH	Park Royal H41/31F	1965
RMF2764-2765	FPT 601-602C	AEC Routemaster 3R2RH	Park Royal H41/31F	1965
RMF2766	FPT 604C	AEC Routemaster 3R2RH	Park Royal H41/31F	1965

RMF2767	EUP 404B	AEC Routemaster 3R2RH	Park Royal H41/31F	1964
RMF2768	RCN 687	AEC Routemaster 3R2RH	Park Royal H41/31F	1964
RMF2769	RCN 696	AEC Routemaster 3R2RH	Park Royal H41/31F	1964
RMF2770	FPT 600C	AEC Routemaster 3R2RH	Park Royal H41/31F	1965
RMF2771	RCN 701	AEC Routemaster 3R2RH	Park Royal H41/31F	1964
RMF2772	RCN 697	AEC Routemaster 3R2RH	Park Royal H41/31F	1964

- These 12 buses were purchased from dealers in 1979-80 and were sold in 1981 without being used.

Former Northern General Routemasters hired from 1979

RMF2791	FPT 589C	AEC Routemaster 3R2RH	Park Royal H41/31F	1964
RMF2792	EUP 407B	AEC Routemaster 3R2RH	Park Royal H41/31F	1964
RMF2793	EUP 406B	AEC Routemaster 3R2RH	Park Royal H41/31F	1964
RMF2794	FPT 588C	AEC Routemaster 3R2RH	Park Royal H41/31F	1964

- These four buses were generally used on sightseeing tours.
- RMF2791/2 were originally numbered RMF2761/2 and were hired from Brakell (dealer), Cheam.
- RMF2793/4 were hired from Obsolete Fleet. RMF2793 was converted to open-top and renumbered RMT2793. It was bought by London Buses in 1987.

The unique rear-engined Routemaster, one of the bus industry's great might-have-beens, was operated by LT from 1967 to 1983. From 1971 to 1976 it was based at Potters Bar, running on local service 284 which needed just one bus. Here it loads at Potters Bar station in December 1974. *Tony Wilson*

Routemasters purchased from British Airways

RMA1	KGJ 621D	RMA18	KGY 618D	RMA35	KGJ 609D	RMA52	NMY 637E
RMA2	NMY 626E	RMA19	KGJ 622D	RMA36	KGJ 610D	RMA53	NMY 641E
RMA3	NMY 627E	RMA20	NMY 633E	RMA37	KGJ 612D	RMA54	NMY 643E
RMA4	NMY 629E	RMA21	NMY 642E	RMA38	KGJ 613D	RMA55	NMY 644E
RMA5	NMY 635E	RMA22	NMY 645E	RMA39	KGJ 615D	RMA56	NMY 651E
RMA6	NMY 638E	RMA23	NMY 649E	RMA40	KGJ 616D	RMA57	NMY 654E
RMA7	NMY 639E	RMA24	NMY 650E	RMA41	KGJ 619D	RMA58	NMY 655E
RMA8	NMY 640E	RMA25	NMY 653E	RMA42	KGJ 620D	RMA59	NMY 657E
RMA9	NMY 646E	RMA26	NMY 660E	RMA43	KGJ 623D	RMA60	NMY 658E
RMA10	NMY 647E	RMA27	NMY 661E	RMA44	KGJ 624D	RMA61	NMY 659E
RMA11	NMY 648E	RMA28	KGJ 601D	RMA45	KGJ 625D	RMA62	NMY 662E
RMA12	NMY 652E	RMA29	KGJ 603D	RMA46	NMY 628E	RMA63	NMY 663E
RMA13	NMY 656E	RMA30	KGJ 604D	RMA47	NMY 630E	RMA64	NMY 664E
RMA14	KGJ 602D	RMA31	KGJ 605D	RMA48	NMY 631E	RMA65	NMY 665E
RMA15	KGJ 611D	RMA32	KGJ 606D	RMA49	NMY 632E		
RMA16	KGJ 614D	RMA33	KGJ 607D	RMA50	NMY 634E		
RMA17	KGJ 617D	RMA34	KGJ 608D	RMA51	NMY 636E		

- RMA1-65 were former BEA buses bought from British Airways between 1975 and 1979.
- RMA1-13 were operated on service 175 (North Romford to Dagenham) in 1975-76. Of the others some were used as staff buses or for driver training while others were scrapped without being used.

RMA2 was one of 13 Routemasters which LT acquired from British Airways in 1975 and which were operated briefly on route 175 between Dagenham and North Romford. By 1978 it was being used on services provided for employees at Aldenham Works. *Tony Wilson*

Unlike later batches of buses which were given liveries to mark special events, the 25 Routemasters repainted silver to mark the Queen's jubilee in 1977 were renumbered, in an SRM series. SRM8, sponsored by the *Daily Mirror*, heads south through Oxford Circus.

Routemasters repainted silver in 1977 to mark the Queen's 25 years on the throne

SRM1	ALD 898B	SRM8	787 DYE	SRM15	ALD 903B	SRM22	ALD 900B
SRM2	848 DYE	SRM9	ALD 907B	SRM16	ALD 920B	SRM23	ALD 902B
SRM3	650 DYE	SRM10	ALD 914B	SRM17	ALD 894B	SRM24	ALD 922B
SRM4	ALD 889B	SRM11	ALD 910B	SRM18	ALD 906B	SRM25	850 DYE
SRM5	668 DYE	SRM12	ALD 911B	SRM19	ALD 904B		
SRM6	ALD 912B	SRM13	648 DYE	SRM20	ALD 899B		
SRM7	ALD 871B	SRM14	ALD 896B	SRM21	ALD 870B		

- SRM1-25 were sponsored by advertisers, including once-familiar businesses like Abbey National, Townsend Thoresen and Woolworths.

Lengthened Routemasters for operation on the Original London Sightseeing Tour

ERM80	VLT 80	ERM94	VLT 94	ERM235	VLT 235	ERM261	VLT 261
ERM84	VLT 84	ERM143	VLT 143	ERM237	VLT 237		
ERM90	VLT 90	ERM163	VLT 163	ERM242	VLT 242		

- The ERMs were standard Routemasters which had been converted to open-top and then had an additional full-length bay added by Kent Engineering in 1990 to make them 32ft 6in long. This allowed the upper deck seating capacity to be increased from 36 to 44 (compared with 40 on a 30ft-long RML), maximising the number of open-air seats.

AEC Reliance

Having purchased 700 sturdy AEC Regal IV buses in 1951-53 London Transport was not in any urgent need of new single-deckers in the first half of the 1960s. It bought small numbers of AEC Reliances – the successor to the Regal IV – for specific tasks, starting with three dual-door vehicles in 1960 to evaluate their use as one-man buses in the Country Area. They had AH470 engines and Willowbrook bodies which were generally similar to those on Reliances being delivered to Grimsby-Cleethorpes Transport. They were sold to Chesterfield Corporation Transport in 1963. During their short lives with LT they were evaluated at five different garages, Hemel Hempstead, Addlestone, Reigate, St Albans and Hertford.

The RW-class AEC Reliances were evaluated at five different Country Area garages between 1960 and 1963. RW1 loads in St Albans in the summer of 1962. *Chris Aston/Omnicolour*

Then in 1965 came 14 Reliances for Green Line service 705, which ran from Sevenoaks to Windsor via central London. They were LT's first 36ft-long vehicles and had AH691 engines, five-speed semi-automatic gearboxes, air suspension – novel in the 1960s – and Willowbrook coach bodies in a livery of pastel grey with a broad green waistband. They passed to London Country Bus Services in January 1970.

The last new Reliances were a further eight with Willowbrook bodies, but now with the AH590 engine. These were operated on behalf of British European Airways and were in BEA Executive Express livery. All were withdrawn in 1974 with four being transferred to British Airways at Glasgow Airport.

London Coaches bought two second-hand Reliances in 1987-88, see page 115.

Specifications

Model	Engine	Displacement	Power output	Gearbox
AEC Reliance RW	AEC AH470	7.7 litres	100bhp	AEC Monocontrol semi-automatic
AEC Reliance RC	AEC AH691	11.3 litres	160bhp	AEC Monocontrol semi-automatic
AEC Reliance EC	AEC AH590	9.6 litres	153bhp	AEC Monocontrol semi-automatic

| RW1-3 | 495-497 ALH | AEC Reliance 2MU3RA | Willowbrook B42D | 1960 |

- These were Country Area buses.

| RC1-14 | CUV 59-72C | AEC Reliance 4U2RA | Willowbrook C49F | 1965 |

- These were Green Line coaches.

| EC1-8 | KHM 1-8D | AEC Reliance 2U3RA | Willowbrook C49F | 1966 |

- These were operated on behalf of BEA.

The Green Line Reliances were in a distinctive grey livery. An anachronism on such a modern coach was the route board displayed above the side windows. These must surely have been the last new coaches in Britain to be fitted with them. RC1 has just crossed the Thames at Windsor on the 48-mile trip to Sevenoaks. Chris Aston/Omnicolour

AEC Merlin and Swift

In 1966 London Transport produced its Bus Reshaping Plan which envisaged the widespread use of high-capacity one-man-operated single-deckers. These were 36ft-long AEC Swifts and were the first of the type to enter service. LT called them Merlins, a name which AEC had intended to use for Swifts with AH691 engines, a model aimed at overseas operators. At best LT's Merlins had a mixed reception since the high capacity was achieved by making most passengers stand. On the 73-passenger standee Merlins there were just 25 seats, all in the raised rear section aft of the centre exit. Standee buses were commonplace in continental Europe, but proved unpopular in London (and elsewhere in Britain) where having paid their fares bus users expected a seat. And the act of paying the fare became more

"London's newest bus" proclaims the banner as an AEC Merlin on a barge demonstrates the imagined future of the capital's transport in 1968. London Bridge is being dismantled for shipment to Lake Havasu City in Arizona. The tug, *William White*, dated from 1919. *Bill Godwin*

One-man operation was introduced to central London in 1966 when six Strachans-bodied AEC Merlins were purchased for new Red Arrow limited-stop service 500. This ran between Victoria Station and Marble Arch with a flat fare of sixpence (2.5p). LT used blue destination blinds on express services. *Geoffrey Morant*

complicated with the use of automatic fare collection whereby passengers were encouraged to use coin-operated turnstiles (also referred to as passimeters) which opened when the correct fare was paid. Such a system might work well enough in railway station toilets, but proved troublesome on moving buses.

The Merlins had a swept turning circle of 71ft and proved awkward to manoeuvre in London traffic, so after ordering 665 Merlins LT opted for a shorter version. This was the 33ft 5in-long Swift, with a 65ft turning circle. Because it had a shorter rear overhang there was insufficient space for the 11.3-litre AH691 engine used in the Merlin, and the 838 Swifts were powered by the smaller 8.2-litre AH505. Both types had AEC Monocontrol automatic transmission.

The Swifts might have been more manoeuvrable, but they were no more popular with passengers. And both the Swifts and Merlins proved unreliable in service. This led to their premature withdrawal, with the first coming out of service as early as 1973. LT's aim was to avoid the expensive overhaul which would be needed on the expiry of the vehicles' initial seven-year Certificate of Fitness. At the end of the 1970s Citybus of Belfast and the associated Ulsterbus business bought 217 redundant Merlins and Swifts, including some which came from London Country. And 58 Swifts were sold to Malta. But few saw further use as buses in Britain.

The 15 original Merlins delivered in 1966 had bodies by Strachans of Hamble, near Southampton. If that company had hoped to win a share of LT's single-deck orders it was in for a disappointment. The 650 production vehicles which followed in 1968-69 were bodied by Metro-Cammell. The bodies for the Swifts, to the same general design, were built by Metro-Cammell (390), Park Royal (323) and Marshall of Cambridge (125). Strachans, no longer a major player in the bus business, closed in 1974.

Total Swift production was around 2,500 chassis, with LT taking 60 per cent of them.

SMS838 was the last AEC for London Transport and the chassis was duly handed over in November 1971 to LT chairman Richard Way by Leyland chairman Lord Stokes. The completed bus entered service in March 1972 and was unceremoniously sold for scrap seven years later – a sad end for a significant bus from the company which had justifiably promoted itself as *Builders of London's Buses* and which over a period of 39 years had supplied LT with some 12,500 chassis.

Specifications

Model	Engine	Displacement	Power output	Gearbox
AEC Merlin	AEC AH691	11.3 litres	166bhp	AEC Monocontrol four-speed automatic
AEC Swift	AEC AH505	8.2 litres	132bhp	AEC Monocontrol four-speed automatic

MB series

XMB1-9	JLA 57-65D	AEC Merlin P2R	Strachans B46D	1966

- These were built as Country Area buses.
- XMB2-9 were not used in the Country Area because the trade union would not accept them as one-man-operated buses. They were rebuilt to Red Arrow specification before entering service in 1967 as XMS7-14.
- XMB1 was renumbered XMB15 in 1966 then re-registered in 1967, first as NHX 15E then as SMM 15F. It did not enter passenger service until 1969. It passed to London Country in 1970 and was bought back by LT in 1973.

XMS1-6	JLA 51-56D	AEC Merlin P2R	Strachans B25+48D	1966
XMS7-14	JLA 58-65D	AEC Merlin P2R	Strachans B25+48D	1966
MBS15	SMM 15F	AEC Merlin P2R	Strachans B46D	1966
MBA16-31	VLW 16-31G	AEC Merlin 3P2R	Metro-Cammell B25+48D	1968
MBS32-35	SMM 32-35F	AEC Merlin 3P2R	Metro-Cammell B25+48D	1968
MBS36	VLW 36G	AEC Merlin 3P2R	Metro-Cammell B25+48D	1968
MBS37-38	SMM 37-38F	AEC Merlin 3P2R	Metro-Cammell B25+48D	1968
MBS39-80	VLW 39-80G	AEC Merlin 3P2R	Metro-Cammell B25+48D	1968
MB81-92	SMM 81-92F	AEC Merlin 3P2R	Metro-Cammell B45D	1968
MB93-96	VLW 93-96G	AEC Merlin 3P2R	Metro-Cammell B45D	1968
MB97	SMM 97F	AEC Merlin 3P2R	Metro-Cammell B45D	1968
MB98-113	VLW 98-113G	AEC Merlin 3P2R	Metro-Cammell B45D	1968
MB114-165	VLW 114-165G	AEC Merlin 3P2R	Metro-Cammell B50F	1968
MBA166-193	VLW 166-193G	AEC Merlin 4P2R	Metro-Cammell B25+48D	1968
MBS194-269	VLW 194-269G	AEC Merlin 4P2R	Metro-Cammell B25+48D	1968
MBS270-303	VLW 270-303G	AEC Merlin 4P2R	Metro-Cammell B25+48D	1968
MB304-397	VLW 303-397G	AEC Merlin 4P2R	Metro-Cammell B50F	1968
MBS398-438	VLW 398-438G	AEC Merlin 4P2R	Metro-Cammell B25+48D	1968
MBS439-546	VLW 438-564G	AEC Merlin 4P2R	Metro-Cammell B25+48D	1968-69
MBS547-615	AML 547-615H	AEC Merlin 4P2R	Metro-Cammell B25+48D	1969
MB616-624	WMT 616-624G	AEC Merlin 4P2R	Metro-Cammell B50F	1969
MB625-665	AML 625-665H	AEC Merlin 4P2R	Metro-Cammell B50F	1969

- XMS7-14 were originally Country Area buses XMB2-9.
- MBS15 was ex London Country in 1973.
- MBA/MBS/MB16-250 were to have been registered SMM 16-250F.
- MBS547-624 were to have been registered VLW 547-624G.
- MB625-635 were to have been registered WMT 625-635G.
- MB81-113, MBS270-303, 398-438 were Country Area buses.
- The 4P2R chassis had a higher driving position than the earlier vehicles.

SM series

SM1-50	AML 1-50H	AEC Swift 4MP2R	Marshall B42F	1969-70
SMS51-100	AML 51-100H	AEC Swift 4MP2R	Park Royal B33+34D	1970
SM101-148	BPH 101-148H	AEC Swift 4MP2R	Park Royal B38+18D	1970
SMS149-223	EGN 149-223J	AEC Swift 4MP2R	Marshall B33+34D	1970-71
SMS224-448	EGN 224-448J	AEC Swift 4MP2R	Park Royal B33+34D	1970-71

Nine Merlins were built for Country Area operation in 1966 but were not immediately used. Eight were rebuilt and repainted for Red Arrow services, entering service in central London 1967. The ninth, the only one to remain green, did not enter service until 1969 and is seen here in 1971 still in LT livery but with London Country fleetnames and logo. It was transferred back to LT in 1973.
The Bus Archive/Peter Henson

The 650 production Merlins and 838 Swifts were all built to this general design, with the Merlins being 36ft long and the Swifts 33ft. SMS277 in Croydon is a 1970 Swift with Park Royal body. It was withdrawn after five years' service. The yellow notice on the front was a simple but effective way of advising passengers this was a one-man-operated bus.

SM449-538	DPD 449-538J	AEC Swift 4MP2R	Metro-Cammell B41+15D	1970-71
SMS539-695	EGN 539-695J	AEC Swift 4MP2R	Metro-Cammell B33+34D	1971
SMS696-838	JGF 696-838K	AEC Swift 4MP2R	Metro-Cammell B33+34D	1971-72

● SM101-148 and SM449-538 were ordered by London Transport but delivered to London Country Bus Services. The LCBS head office was in Reigate, hence the Surrey registration marks

Experimental double-deckers 1965

For all its technical sophistication, the front-engined rear-entrance Routemaster was being overtaken by events. In most other big cities in the UK – for example, Belfast, Birmingham, Glasgow, Liverpool, Newcastle upon Tyne and Nottingham – no rear-entrance buses were added to their fleets after 1960. Urban bus operators, sometimes with a measure of justifiable hesitation, were switching to front-entrance rear-engined models.

In 1964 London Transport ordered 50 Leyland Atlanteans for Central Area services and eight Daimler Fleetlines for the Country Area. The Fleetlines were unusual in being fitted with

The 50 Atlanteans and eight Fleetlines delivered in 1965-66 had this style of Park Royal bodywork. In the summer of 1966 XA12 was one of a large number of Atlanteans based at Tottenham garage and used on the 76 to Victoria.
Iain MacGregor

a door at the bottom of the stairs which could be closed at off-peak periods to allow the bus to be one-man-operated as if it were a single-decker; double-deck one-man operation was not legal when the order was placed. And in London the emphasis was firmly on one-*man* operation; until 1973 the unions blocked the employment of women as bus drivers at LT.

All 58 buses had plain-looking Park Royal bodies at a time when other builders had shown that rear-engined buses needn't look boxy. Metro-Cammell bodies for Liverpool and Alexander bodies for Glasgow set trends which London chose not to follow. But LT did at least specify fairings above the engine to disguise the notch effect of the engine compartment.

The eight Fleetlines were the first rear-engined double-deckers in LT service when they took to the road from East Grinstead garage on the 424 to Reigate in September 1965. They were also LT's first new Gardner-engined buses since the last of the Guy Arab IIs in 1946, and were reported to be returning 10.6mpg on the 424. They were taken over by London Country Bus Services in January 1970.

The first Atlanteans entered service in November 1965 at Chalk Farm garage on service 24, Hampstead Heath to Pimlico. All 50 Atlanteans were sold to China Motor Bus, Hong Kong, in 1973.

Specifications

Model	Engine	Displacement	Power output	Gearbox
Atlantean PDR1/1	Leyland O.680	11.1 litres	130bhp	Pneumocyclic four-speed automatic
Fleetline CRG6LX	Gardner 6LX	10.45 litres	140bhp	Daimatic four-speed semi-automatic

XA

| XA1-37 | CUV 1-37C | Leyland Atlantean PDR1/1 | Park Royal H41/31F | 1965 |
| XA38-50 | JLA 38-50D | Leyland Atlantean PDR1/1 | Park Royal H41/31F | 1966 |

- XA1-50 were to have been registered CUV 1-50C.

XF

| XF1-8 | CUV 51-58C | Daimler Fleetline CRG6LX | Park Royal H43/31F | 1965 |

- XF1-8 were Country Area buses and were taken over by London Country Bus Services in January 1970.

At the end of 1969 LT repainted three Daimler Fleetlines in Blue Arrow livery for a service in Stevenage which started on 29 December, just three days before LT's Country Area operations were taken over by London Country on 1 January 1970. They carried London Country fleetnames from the outset. *Geoffrey Morant*

Daimler/Leyland Fleetline

London Transport started evaluating 50 Leyland Atlanteans and eight Daimler Fleetlines in 1965. When in 1969 it decided to order one-man-operated rear-engined double-deckers it went to Daimler, with an initial requirement for 17 Fleetlines, soon increased to 117, and then to 367. The biggest single order for Fleetlines followed in 1971 when LT placed an order for 1,600 chassis, worth £18.5million. A final order, for 679, was placed in 1974. This took the total to 2,646, accounting for almost one quarter of total Fleetline production.

When the Fleetlines were launched by LT in January 1971 they were given the name Londoner, but that didn't catch on and was almost immediately forgotten. They were 9m

Brand new Fleetline DMS1384 leans over as it pulls out of West Croydon bus station at the start of 1973. It had a Leyland O.680 engine and a Metro-Cammell body and only served six years in London. The adult fare on the C3 express to New Addington was 10p.

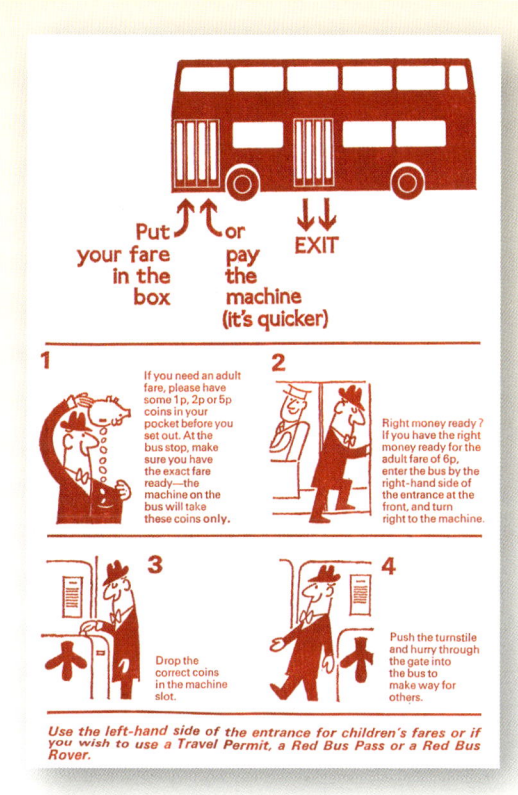

Put ↑↑ or ↑↑ pay EXIT your fare the in the machine box (it's quicker)

1 If you need an adult fare, please have some 1p, 2p or 5p coins in your pocket before you set out. At the bus stop, make sure you have the exact fare ready—the machine on the bus will take these coins only.

2 Right money ready? If you have the right money ready for the adult fare of 6p, enter the bus by the right-hand side of the entrance at the front, and turn right to the machine.

3 Drop the correct coins in the machine slot.

4 Push the turnstile and hurry through the gate into the bus to make way for others.

Use the left-hand side of the entrance for children's fares or if you wish to use a Travel Permit, a Red Bus Pass or a Red Bus Rover.

Between 1968 and 1979 LT was of the view that turnstiles on high-capacity one-man-operated buses would reduce boarding times. This 1975 leaflet tries to convince passengers that automatic fare collection is a good idea. In the early days the system was used in conjunction with a 6d (2½p) flat fare which could be paid by a single coin. In 1975 the flat fare routes were charging 6p and this needed a minimum of two coins which complicated the process of fare payment.

(30ft 10in) long, and the dual-door bodies were built by Park Royal and Metro-Cammell, both to the same design which was derived from a style introduced by Park Royal in 1968. It was certainly a more attractive body than that fitted to the 1965 buses, with much bigger windows, but it wasn't a head-turner. The all-over red livery didn't help.

The new Fleetlines had 68 seats and room for 21 standing passengers. They were classified DMS, and the first routes on which they operated were the 95 from Cannon Street Station to Tooting Broadway, operated by Brixton garage, and the 220 from Harlesden to Tooting which was operated by Shepherds Bush. Between 1974 and 1978 there were 460 Fleetlines delivered which were intended for crew operation and these were coded DM. Because they lacked the automatic fare collection equipment fitted to the one-man buses they had three more seats in the lower saloon.

LT's optimistic aim when it introduced the Fleetlines was that all of its bus services would be one-man-operated by 1977. That meant the newest Routemasters would have been withdrawn when they were just nine years old. But that didn't work out.

Daimler had been part of the British Motor Corporation since 1966, and BMC was merged with Leyland two years later to create the British Leyland Motor Corporation. Change was in the air. In 1970 the Leyland O.680 engine was offered in the Fleetline as an alternative to the original Gardner unit, and in 1973 Fleetline chassis production was moved from Coventry to Leyland. The first Leyland-built Fleetline chassis was for LT, entering service in January 1974 as DMS742.

LT's final 400 Fleetlines, the B20 variant, were fitted with turbocharged Leyland 690 engines and a revised engine enclosure designed to reduce noise. After ten years' operation 201 surviving B20s were re-powered with 8.1-litre Iveco 8361 engines.

After the fiasco of the Swift and Merlin single-deckers, LT had another perceived failure on its hands with the Fleetline, with the first examples being withdrawn as the last were being delivered. The Fleetline was complex. It was less reliable than the Routemaster. In a 1979 interview with *Commercial Motor*, LT managing director (buses) David Quarmby noted that even allowing for the cost of crew operation, Routemasters were more economical than

Fleetlines. They used less fuel – about 11mpg compared with 6.5mpg – and because they were more reliable the figure for engineering spares was just 5.5 per cent, less than half the 12.5 to 15 per cent needed for Fleetlines.

Yet large numbers of Fleetlines which couldn't work in London found new owners not just around Britain, but also in the arduous operating environment of Hong Kong. And in 1987 London Buses actually bought back 14 DMSs from Clydeside Scottish, using them on Bexleybus services. So perhaps the much maligned Fleetline wasn't so bad after all. Indeed, in a 1984 interview with *Commercial Motor*, Quarmby admitted: "Although the Fleetline did have some problems with us, it was our inability to respond to different maintenance needs which caused most trouble."

The regular operation of Fleetlines on scheduled service ended in 1992. In addition to the 2,646 bought new (plus the eight XF-class buses) LT also purchased seven convertible open-top Fleetlines from Bournemouth Transport in 1977 for the Round London Sightseeing Tour.

Specifications

Model	Engine	Displacement	Power output
CRG6LX (DMO)	Gardner 6LX	10.45 litres	150bhp
CRG6LXB	Gardner 6LXB	10.45 litres	170bhp
CRL6	Leyland O.680	11.1 litres	170bhp
FE30AGR	Gardner 6LXB	10.45 litres	170bhp
FE30ALR	Leyland O.680	11.1 litres	170bhp
FE30ALR B20	Leyland 690	11.1 litres	163bhp

- Rolls-Royce Eagle 12.2 litre engines were fitted to DMS864, DM1199, DMS1968, 2059, 2120.

DMS1-131	EGP 1-131J	Daimler Fleetline CRG6LXB	Park Royal H44/24D	1970-71
DMS132	EGP 132J	Daimler Fleetline CRL6	Park Royal H44/24D	1971
DMS133-136	EGP 133-136J	Daimler Fleetline CRG6LXB	Park Royal H44/24D	1971
DMS137-414	JGF 137-414K	Daimler Fleetline CRG6LXB	Park Royal H44/24D	1971-72
DMS415-494	MLK 415-494L	Daimler Fleetline CRG6LXB	Park Royal H44/24D	1972
DMS495-607	MLK 495-607L	Daimler Fleetline CRL6	Park Royal H44/24D	1972-73
DMS608-611	MLK 608-611L	Daimler Fleetline CRG6LXB	Park Royal H44/24D	1973
DMS612-616	MLK 612-616L	Daimler Fleetline CRL6	Park Royal H44/24D	1973
DMS617-619	MLK 617-619L	Daimler Fleetline CRG6LXB	Park Royal H44/24D	1973
DMS620-636	MLK 620-636L	Daimler Fleetline CRL6	Park Royal H44/24D	1973
DMS637-639	MLK 637-639L	Daimler Fleetline CRG6LXB	Park Royal H44/24D	1973
DMS640-654	MLK 640-654L	Daimler Fleetline CRL6	Park Royal H44/24D	1973
DMS655	MLK 655L	Daimler Fleetline CRG6LXB	Park Royal H44/24D	1973
DMS656-658	MLK 656-658L	Daimler Fleetline CRL6	Park Royal H44/24D	1973
DMS659-660	MLK 659-660L	Daimler Fleetline CRG6LXB	Park Royal H44/24D	1973
DMS661-695	MLK 661-695L	Daimler Fleetline CRL6	Park Royal H44/24D	1973
DMS696-900	TGX 696-900M	Daimler Fleetline CRL6	Park Royal H44/24D	1973-74
DMS901-917	SMU 901-917N	Daimler Fleetline CRL6	Park Royal H44/24D	1974
DM918-947	SMU 918-947N	Daimler Fleetline CRL6	Park Royal H44/27D	1974
DM948-999	GHV 948-999N	Daimler Fleetline CRL6	Park Royal H44/27D	1974
DM1000	GHV 500N	Daimler Fleetline CRL6	Park Royal H44/27D	1974
DM1001-1014	GHV 1-124N	Daimler Fleetline CRL6	Park Royal H44/27D	1974-75
DM1125-1217	KUC 125-217P	Daimler Fleetline CRL6	Park Royal H44/27D	1975-6
DM1218-1247	KUC 218-247P	Daimler Fleetline CRL6	Metro-Cammell H44/27D	1976
DMS1248-1249	JGU 248-249K	Daimler Fleetline CRG6LXB	Metro-Cammell H44/24D	1972

DMS1250	JGU 250K	Daimler Fleetline CRL6	Metro-Cammell H44/24D	1972
DMS1251-1297	JGU 251-297K	Daimler Fleetline CRG6LXB	Metro-Cammell H44/24D	1972
DMS1298-1371	MLH 298-371L	Daimler Fleetline CRG6LXB	Metro-Cammell H44/24D	1972
DMS1372-1451	MLH 372-451L	Daimler Fleetline CRL6	Metro-Cammell H44/24D	1972-73
DMS1452-1467	MLH 452-467L	Daimler Fleetline CRG6LXB	Metro-Cammell H44/24D	1973
DMS1468-1499	MLH 468-499L	Daimler Fleetline CRL6	Metro-Cammell H44/24D	1973
DMS1500-1702	THM 500-702M	Daimler Fleetline CRL6	Metro-Cammell H44/24D	1973-74
DM1703-1720	THM 703-720M	Daimler Fleetline CRL6	Metro-Cammell H44/27D	1974
DM1721-1739	SMU 721-739N	Daimler Fleetline CRL6	Metro-Cammell H44/27D	1974
DM1740-1832	GHM 740-832N	Daimler Fleetline CRL6	Metro-Cammell H44/27D	1974-75
DMS1833-1897	GHM 833-897N	Daimler Fleetline CRL6	Metro-Cammell H44/24D	1975
DMS1898-1967	KUC 898-967P	Daimler Fleetline CRL6	Metro-Cammell H44/24D	1975
DMS1968-1999	KUC 968-999P	Leyland Fleetline FE30ALR	Metro-Cammell H44/24D	1976
DMS2000	KJD 500P	Leyland Fleetline FE30ALR	Metro-Cammell H44/24D	1976
DMS2001-2024	KJD 1-24P	Leyland Fleetline FE30ALR	Metro-Cammell H44/24D	1976
DMS2025-2037	OUC 25-37R	Leyland Fleetline FE30ALR	Metro-Cammell H44/24D	1976
DMS2038-2057	OUC 38-57R	Leyland Fleetline FE30AGR	Metro-Cammell H44/24D	1976
DMS2058-2122	KJD 58-122P	Leyland Fleetline FE30ALR	Park Royal H44/24D	1976
DMS2121-2122	KJD 121-122P	Leyland Fleetline FE30ALR	Park Royal H44/24D	1976
DMS2123-2127	OJD 123-127R	Leyland Fleetline FE30ALR	Park Royal H44/24D	1976
DMS2128-2166	OJD 128-166R	Leyland Fleetline FE30AGR	Park Royal H44/24D	1976-77
DMS2167-2246	OJD 167-246R	Leyland Fleetline FE30AGR	Metro-Cammell H44/24D	1976-77
DMS2247-2267	OJD 247-267R	Leyland Fleetline FE30ALRSp	Metro-Cammell H44/24D	1977
DMS2268-2346	THX 268-346S	Leyland Fleetline FE30ALRSp	Metro-Cammell H44/24D	1977-78
DMS2347-2472	OJD 347-472R	Leyland Fleetline FE30ALRSp	Park Royal H44/24D	1977
DMS2473-2526	THX 473-526S	Leyland Fleetline FE30ALRSp	Park Royal H44/24D	1977
DM2527-2646	THX 527-646S	Leyland Fleetline FE30ALRSp	Park Royal H44/27D	1977-78

- DMS854 had a Leyland 690 engine and was the prototype B20 Fleetline.
- DMS2247-2646 were B20 models.

Fleetlines purchased from Bournemouth Transport in 1977

DMO1-6	CRU 182-187C	Daimler Fleetline CRG6LX	Weymann CO43/31F	1965
DMO7	CRU 189C	Daimler Fleetline CRG6LX	Weymann CO43/31F	1965

- DMO1-7 were operated on the Round London Sightseeing Tour until 1981.

Fleetlines purchased from Clydeside Scottish Omnibuses in 1987

DMS1492	MLH 492L	Daimler Fleetline CRL6	Metro-Cammell H44/33F	1973
DMS1580	THM 580M	Daimler Fleetline CRL6	Metro-Cammell H44/33F	1973
DMS1610	THM 610M	Daimler Fleetline CRL6	Metro-Cammell H44/33F	1974
DMS1649	THM 649M	Daimler Fleetline CRL6	Metro-Cammell H44/33F	1974
DMS1656-1657	THM 656-657M	Daimler Fleetline CRL6	Metro-Cammell H44/33F	1974
DMS1669-1671	THM 659-671M	Daimler Fleetline CRL6	Metro-Cammell H44/33F	1974
DMS1679	THM 679M	Daimler Fleetline CRL6	Metro-Cammell H44/33F	1974
DMS1683	THM 683M	Daimler Fleetline CRL6	Metro-Cammell H44/33F	1974
DMS1686-1687	THM 686-687M	Daimler Fleetline CRL6	Metro-Cammell H44/33F	1974
DMS2021	KJD 21P	Leyland Fleetline FE30ALR	Metro-Cammell H44/33F	1976

- These were numbered 77-90 in the Bexleybus fleet. They had been bought from LT by Western SMT between 1981 and 1984, passing to Clydeside in 1985.

Leyland National

The Leyland National was a joint project between British Leyland and the National Bus Company. It was a highly-standardised integral single-decker built using production methods more like those of the car industry than traditional bus manufacturing. It was unveiled at the 1970 Commercial Motor Show and production started in 1972 in a new purpose-designed factory in Workington, Cumberland.

The original model used Leyland's 8.2-litre fixed-head 510 turbocharged engine, which proved not to be popular with bus engineers and was replaced in 1979 by the 11.1-litre 680, at which point the bus became the National 2. To accommodate the bigger engine the radiator on the National 2 was relocated from the rear to the front, increasing the overall

LS7, the first of LT's bulk National deliveries, was used on the front cover of Leyland's 1976 sales brochure. Route 285 did serve Hatton Cross Station, but was operated by double-deckers and never ran anywhere near Westminster. Models seldom manage to look like real bus passengers, and the young lady boarding LS7 is no exception. *Gavin Booth collection*

A fleet of 69 National 2s delivered in 1981 replaced AEC Merlins on Red Arrow services. The basic National structure was unchanged from the original model but the front end was extended by 300mm to accommodate the radiator which had previously been at the rear. LS493 is at Euston Station. *Tony Wilson*

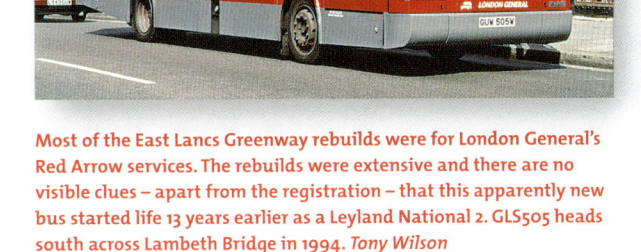

Most of the East Lancs Greenway rebuilds were for London General's Red Arrow services. The rebuilds were extensive and there are no visible clues – apart from the registration – that this apparently new bus started life 13 years earlier as a Leyland National 2. GLS505 heads south across Lambeth Bridge in 1994. *Tony Wilson*

length of the bus from 10.3 to 10.6 metres. The National 2 had Leyland's Hydracyclic gearbox which had an integral retarder.

London Transport took six Nationals in 1973, for comparison with six Metro-Scanias. A further 51 were ordered in 1976 to boost fleet replacement at a time when there were delays in the delivery of new Fleetline double-deckers. The National factory was working well below its planned capacity and was able to offer quick delivery. By 1979 there were 437 examples of the original National in the LT fleet. These were followed in 1981 by 69 National 2s to replace AEC Merlins on Red Arrow services.

During the lean years for new bus orders in the early 1990s, East Lancashire Coachbuilders of Blackburn embarked on a programme of refurbishing Leyland Nationals, marketing the extensively rebuilt product as the Greenway. Two Nationals were rebuilt as Greenways for London Buses in the autumn of 1992. They created a good impression and a further 41 National 2s were rebuilt by East Lancs in 1993-94 for continued use by London General on Red Arrow routes. All were converted from Leyland to Gardner engines, and from Hydracyclic to ZF gearboxes. They retained their original fleetnumbers but with a new GLS type code. The rebuild altered the character of the vehicles, and extended their lives quite significantly. The Greenways would operate on Red Arrow services until 2002 by which time the original National structure was over 20 years old.

Two second-hand Nationals were purchased in 1990-91 for use on dedicated mobility services for disabled people. They differed from those bought new by LT in being 11.3m long, hence the LSL (for Long) type code. They had wheelchair lifts fitted in the centre door to provide access for passengers with impaired mobility.

LS1-6	TGY 101-106M	Leyland National 1051/2R	B36+29D	1973
LS7-57	KJD 507-557P	Leyland National 10351A/2R	B36+27D	1976
LS58-107	OJD 858-907R	Leyland National 10351A/2R	B36+27D	1977
LS108-267	THX 108-267S	Leyland National 10351A/2R	B36+27D	1977-78
LS268-297	YYE 268-297S	Leyland National 10351A/2R	B36+27D	1978-79
LS298-355	AYR 298-355T	Leyland National 10351A/2R	B36+27D	1979
LS356-437	BYW 356-437V	Leyland National 10351A/2R	B36+27D	1979
LS438-506	GUW 438-506W	Leyland National 2 NL106AL11/2R	B24+46D	1981

- LS1-6 were to have been registered MYK 101-106L.
- LS438-506 were Red Arrow vehicles.

East Lancs Greenway rebuilds of Leyland National 2s, 1992-94

GLS1	GUW 466W	GLS463	WLT 463	GLS487	WLT 487
GLS2	FCA 9X	GLS467	WLT 467	GLS490	GUW 490W
GLS438	GUW 438W	GLS468	GUW 468W	GLS491	GUW 491W
GLS439	GUW 439W	GLS469	GUW 469W	GLS492	GUW 492W
GLS440	GUW 440W	GLS471	GUW 471W	GLS493	GUW 493W
GLS442	GUW 442W	GLS473	GUW 473W	GLS496	WLT 696
GLS443	WLT 843	GLS474	GUW 474W	GLS498	WLT 598
GLS446	GUW 446W	GLS476	GUW 476W	GLS499	WLT 599
GLS448	WLT 648	GLS477	GUW 477W	GLS500	GUW 500W
GLS449	GUW 449W	GLS478	GUW 478W	GLS501	GUW 501W
GLS450	GUW 450W	GLS479	GUW 479W	GLS502	GUW 502W
GLS452	GUW 452W	GLS480	VLT 180	GLS505	GUW 505W
GLS455	GUW 455W	GLS481	GUW 481W	GLS506	GUW 506W
GLS459	GUW459W	GLS483	83 CLT		
GLS460	GUW 460W	GLS486	186 CLT		

- GLS1 was a rebuild of LS466. All of the other Greenways apart from GLS2 retained their original fleetnumbers but with a GLS prefix.
- GLS2 was a rebuild of a bus which had been new to Crosville Motor Services. It was based on an 11.6m-long National and was operated by CentreWest. Unlike the other London Greenways it was a single-door bus. It was re-registered 292 CLT soon after entering service.

Leyland Nationals purchased for mobility services

LSL1	WYJ 165S	Leyland National 11351A/2R	B25DL	1978
LSL2	RUF 42R	Leyland National 11351A/2R	B25DL	1977

- LSL1 ex Southdown Motor Services, 1990.
- LSL2 ex Topline, Hastings, 1991. LSL2 was operated by Kentish Bus in London Buses red and yellow mobility bus livery.

Specifications

Model	Engine	Displacement	Power output	Gearbox
National	Leyland 510	8.2 litres	150bhp	Leyland Pneumocyclic
National 2	Leyland 680	11.1 litres	170bhp	Leyland Hydracyclic
Greenway	Gardner 6HLXB	10.45 litres	170bhp	ZF 4HP500 automatic

For operation on mobility services London Buses purchased two second-hand Leyland Nationals and also adapted a number of Nationals in its existing fleet. The key feature was the provision of a wheelchair lift in the centre doorway. This drawing is from a 1992 timetable leaflet.

Bristol LH

The Eastern Coach Works-bodied Bristol LH was the National Bus Company's standard rural bus in the 1970s. Powered by a horizontal 6.54-litre Leyland O.401 engine, those which formed London Transport's BL class were unusual in having epicyclic gearboxes; most LHs had manual gearboxes. They were 30ft long and 7ft 6in wide and replaced RF class AEC Regal IVs. A clue that they were not in the same class as the RFs can be found in the fact that although they were the same size, a BL was almost two tons lighter.

As well as buying standard 30ft-long LHs London Transport also purchased 17 of the compact LHS model. These were just 24ft long (a standard NBC LHS was 26ft 5in) and were bought to replace Ford Transits. Unlike the bigger BL-class buses, BS1-17 had five-speed

This pretty postcard was produced by London Transport in 1976 and shows BS2, one of the compact Bristol LHS6Ls, in leafy north London suburbia on the C11, Highgate to Cricklewood Broadway. The 25-seat Bristols had replaced 16-seat Ford Transits. The bigger BL-class LHs were similar in appearance, but six feet longer.

Later in their lives a few LHs received a predominantly red livery as seen on Metroline BL80 at Arnos Grove on the 251 from Edgware. The Bristols had replaced RF class AEC Regal IVs in 1977 and would in turn be replaced by Dennis Darts shortly after this photo was taken in 1990. Peter Rowlands

synchromesh gearboxes with first gear blanked off. They had short lives in London; all 17 were withdrawn in 1981.

The LHs were delivered in an attractive livery which featured white for the window surrounds and waistband, apart from BL93-95 which had yellow in place of the white and were operated on service 128, Ruislip Station to Harefield Hospital, with support from the London Borough of Hillingdon.

Specifications

Model	Engine	Displacement	Power output	Gearbox
LH6L	Leyland O.401	6.54 litres	125bhp	SCG four-speed semi-automatic
LHS6L	Leyland O.401	6.54 litres	125bhp	Turner five-speed synchromesh

BL1-40	KJD 401-440P	Bristol LH6L	ECW B39F	1976
BL41-95	OJD 41-95R	Bristol LH6L	ECW B39F	1976-77
BS1-6	GHV 501-506N	Bristol LHS6L	ECW B25F	1975
BS7-17	OJD 7-17R	Bristol LHS6L	ECW B25F	1976

Miscellaneous double-deckers

| TT1-5 | 526-530 FJJ | Thames Trader 570E | Strachans H33/0F | 1963 |

- These buses were owned by the Dartford Tunnel Joint Committee and were built to carry up to 30 bicycles through the tunnel which opened in November 1963. They were in Country Area green. The service saw little use and the buses were withdrawn in 1965 and replaced by Land Rovers towing trailers. The Thames Trader 570E was a popular coach chassis and was chosen by LT because it had since 1960 standardised on Thames Trader lorries for its service fleet. Compared with the standard 570E coach the chassis on the LT vehicles had altered springs and a different front axle which lowered the frame height by 4½in allowing the buses to meet the requirements of the Ministry of Transport tilt test.

AEC Regent ST922 had been new to Tillings in 1930. It served LT as a bus until 1946 and then as a mobile canteen until 1954. It was rescued from a scrapyard by pioneer bus preservationist Prince Marshall in 1966, and between 1972 and 1979 was in regular use in central London, primarily on tourist service 100. This is Parliament Square. *Tony Wilson*

The BMMO D9 was built by Midland Red, England's second-biggest bus operator after LT, and could be viewed as the Midlands equivalent of London's Routemaster. It was an integral with an aluminium structure, a low bonnet line, independent front suspension and, initially, front disc brakes. Eight were operated in LT colours by Obsolete Fleet in the late 1970s, usually on the Round London Sightseeing Tour. OM3, new in 1961, negotiates the traffic at Hyde Park Corner. *Tony Wilson*

D142	XX 9591	Dennis 4-ton	Dodson O24/24RO	1925
ST922	GJ 2098	AEC Regent 661	Tilling H27/25RO	1930

- These preserved petrol-engined double-deckers were operated in London colours by Obsolete Fleet in the 1970s.
- D142 had a chassis which had been new to the Dominion Omnibus Co in 1925. It had been repainted in London General colours and was used occasionally on LT sightseeing tours.
- ST922 been new to Thomas Tilling and was used regularly on circular tourist route 100 from Trafalgar Square between 1972 and 1979.

OM1	903 KHA	BMMO D9	BMMO O40/32RD	1961
OM2	6301 HA	BMMO D9	BMMO O40/32RD	1963
OM3	2959 HA	BMMO D9	BMMO O40/32RD	1961
OM4	3043 HA	BMMO D9	BMMO O40/32RD	1963
OM5	3016 HA	BMMO D9	BMMO O40/32RD	1962
OM6	3035 HA	BMMO D9	BMMO O40/32RD	1963
OM7	917 KHA	BMMO D9	BMMO O40/32RD	1961
BM8	6341 HA	BMMO D9	BMMO H40/32RD	1963

- These buses were operated in London red by Obsolete Fleet on the Round London Sightseeing Tour from 1975. They were ex Midland Red (the trading name of the Birmingham & Midland Motor Omnibus Co). The D9 was powered by a 10.5-litre engine of BMMO manufacture.

DRO1	507 RUO	AEC Regent V 2D3RA	Willowbrook OH39/30F	1964
DR3	GJG 750D	AEC Regent V 2D3RA	Park Royal H40/32F	1966

- DRO1 was operated by Obsolete Fleet in London red in 1979 on service 74Z, Baker Street Station to London Zoo. It was ex Devon General.
- DR3 was operated by Obsolete Fleet in London red on the Round London Sightseeing Tour in 1981-82. It had been new to East Kent. It would join Leaside Travel as RV1 in 1991.

82 MISCELLANEOUS DOUBLE-DECKERS

| LE1 | AED 26B | Leyland Titan PD2/40 | East Lancs H37/28R | 1964 |
| LM2 | MCO 669 | Leyland Titan PD2/12 | Metro-Cammell Orion H30/26R | 1956 |

- LE1 and LM2 were used as training vehicles by London Coaches. Both were repainted red with traditional London Transport underlined fleetnames.
- LE1 was bought from a preservationist in 1986. It had been new to Warrington Corporation.
- LM2 was operated on hire in 1988. It had been new to Plymouth Corporation.

| RV1 | GJG 750D | AEC Regent V 2D3RA | Park Royal H40/32F | 1966 |

- RV1 was bought by Leaside Travel from Wealden PSV in 1991 for training and private hire work. It had been operated by Obsolete Fleet as DR3 in the early 1980s.

Leaside Buses RV1 was a former East Kent AEC Regent V with Park Royal body, new in 1966. Here it is providing an Underground replacement service as an extra on route 38 in the summer of 1993. Tony Wilson

MISCELLANEOUS DOUBLE-DECKERS **83**

The Dartford Tunnel Thames bicycle buses were unlikely-looking vehicles. They loaded and unloaded at platforms at either end of the tunnel with bikes being wheeled on to the racks in the centre of the bus, as demonstrated by two very smartly dressed young ladies. Riders then climbed a precarious-looking staircase to take their seats on the top deck. There were staircases on both sides of the bus, and the absence of a door to stop passengers falling out if they missed their footing would surely cause apoplexy among modern day health and safety legislators.

XRM and other unrealised projects

In 1975 London Transport – unhappy with its recent bus purchases – confirmed that its development engineers were considering alternative double-deck designs, one of which would incorporate a side-mounted engine under the staircase, echoing the layout of the AEC Q of the 1930s. This would improve weight distribution and drawing on LT's experience with the Routemaster would be an integral with a low unladen weight. The engine location would allow the provision of an open rear platform, a feature which no forward-thinking bus operator would have countenanced but which, as history would show, would pop up again in London almost 40 years later.

OPPOSITE AND RIGHT: LT produced drawings showing the general appearance of the XRM, and they form the basis of these two illustrations by transport artist Chris Drew. The originals are undated, but the older of the two (opposite page) shows how the eight-wheeler would have looked. The tumblehome at skirt level softens the overall appearance of the body. It uses curved windscreens similar to those fitted to the DMS-class Fleetlines and the AEC Merlins and Swifts before them. The drawing shows flush-fitting doors; that could point to using plug-type doors or it might just have been artistic licence.

The later drawing (above right) of a short two-axle bus featured windscreens with flat glass, angled back to reduce reflections from the interior lighting. The original drawing was captioned "XRM lightweight bus".

LEFT: The original LT drawing for the eight-wheeled XRM.

The new bus was given the type code XRM. One avenue being explored was the use of four axles fitted with smaller wheels and tyres than those used on existing double-deckers. A four-axle urban bus might sound an unlikely concept, but LT was in fact following in the footsteps of Leyland's 1967 Commutabus mock-up which can be viewed as a precursor to the Leyland National. There never were any four-axle buses in Britain, but there was a three-axle model in the 1960s, the Bedford VAL. This had 16-inch wheels, compared with 20 inches on a Daimler Fleetline. The use of smaller wheels would reduce the height of the floor of the XRM, improving accessibility for passengers. LT bought an eight-year-old Bedford VAL coach in 1975 to examine its twin-steer layout.

The XRM was to use a hydrostatic transmission in which the engine powered a pump which supplied pressurised hydraulic fluid to traction motors in the vehicle's wheel hubs. This dispensed with the conventional propeller shaft. The National Engineering Laboratory in East Kilbride was carrying out trials with hydrostatic drives in the 1970s and in 1976 LT sent 18-month-old Fleetline DM1787 to the NEL to have it converted to hydrostatic drive. It was not operated in service and test results at Chiswick were clearly not very good. As development progressed the hydrostatic drive was abandoned and as a consequence the focus switched to a conventional two-axle layout.

Towards the end of the project there were two versions under consideration, an 8.75m two-door 66-seater and a 9.5m two-door 74-seater. The target unladen weight for the shorter model, intended for operation in congested central London, was just 7½ tons at a time when the admittedly bigger DMS-type Fleetline weighed over 9½ tons.

86 XRM AND OTHER UNREALISED PROJECTS

The XRM project was abandoned at the end of 1980 when LT concluded that it would be too expensive to pursue and that there were only marginal benefits to be gained from its side-engined layout.

The end of the XRM did not spell the end of LT's ambitions to procure better buses. In 1985 LT commissioned Ogle Design to come up with some thoughts on the shape of future buses. Ogle produced a stylish full-size mock-up at a cost of £250,000 at a time when a real double-deck bus cost around £80,000. It had a deep, curved, nearside corner window to give the driver a good view of the kerb, and was intended to demonstrate features which would make bus use easier for people with impaired mobility. These included a split-step entrance to ease boarding and alighting, and a straight staircase. The destination screen was offset to the nearside. The split-step arrangement would appear on future London buses and so too, eventually, would the straight staircase.

If the XRM and the Ogle mock-up looked to the future, the final unrealised project looked to the past. London Buses wanted a new Routemaster. It approached a number of manufacturers to test the feasibility of resurrecting the concept of an open-platform rear-entrance bus. These included DAF, truck maker ERF which built rugged front-engined single-deck buses for Africa, and Dennis. Dennis examined the possibility of building a chassis with 5.88-litre Cummins C-series engine (as used in the Dart midibus), ZF automatic gearbox and air suspension.

Alexander and Northern Counties went as far as producing drawings for a half-cab version of their standard aluminium-framed bodies. But with low production volumes the project did not make economic sense and it was abandoned in 1991. Instead of buying new Routemasters London Buses invested in upgrading old ones, notably by fitting them with Cummins and Iveco engines.

The 1985 Ogle mock-up featured a deep glazed corner panel ahead of a split-step entrance.

This illustration is based on a Northern Counties drawing which showed the style of body the company proposed for London Buses' 1990 Routemaster project. The bonnet was hinged vertically behind the front wheel so that it could be swung outwards to give access to the engine. An alternative drawing offered a split-step entrance. Chris Drew has added colour to Northern Counties' black-and-white drawing.

MCW

In 1969 MCW announced that it was working with Swedish manufacturer Scania-Vabis to build an 11m-long single-deck city bus based on Scania's CR110 integral. It may not be coincidence that the announcement came just weeks after Leyland had revealed its plans to build the integral National.

In the event the new model, the Metro-Scania, was not a great success. The six supplied to London Transport in the summer of 1973 for comparison with six Leyland Nationals were the last of just 133 built. The Metro-Scania had air suspension, a rear-mounted Scania 11-litre engine and Scania's own automatic gearbox. The six owned by LT were withdrawn in 1976; after languishing in store for two years five saw further service with Newport Transport from 1978.

LT operated six Metro-Scanias between 1973 and 1976. They ran alongside the original six Leyland Nationals on the S2 between Clapton Pond and Bromley Station. MS4 has just left Clapton Pond terminus in 1974.

The Metropolitans were based in south-east London garages. MD154 is in Piccadilly Circus in 1977 on the 53 which ran from Plumstead to Camden Town. It was one of 21 Metropolitans sold to Reading Transport in 1983. *Gavin Booth*

Between 1976 and 1979 this attractive livery was applied to 528 new double-deckers – 278 Fleetlines, 164 Metropolitans, 55 Metrobuses and 31 Titans. Metrobus M15 is in central Richmond in 1979. The little car heading away from the camera is a Fiat 126, which was powered, or perhaps underpowered, by a rear-mounted two-cylinder 23bhp 600cc engine.

In 1987-88 London Buses bought 14 second-hand Metrobuses which were initially based at Potters Bar for services operating under the new LRT tendered regime. The newest were two 1983 Metrobus IIs from Yorkshire Rider; this is M1440.

Rather more successful in terms of sales was the next MCW-Scania joint venture, the double-deck Metropolitan which used Scania BR111DH running units. This appeared in 1973 and was in production until 1978. London Transport was the biggest customer, taking 164 out of a production run of 659. They were ordered partly to compensate for delayed Fleetline deliveries. The Metropolitan was heavy on fuel and its steel structure was prone to severe corrosion and in London, as elsewhere, they had short lives. All were withdrawn by 1982.

Undeterred by the problems of the Metropolitan MCW developed an all-new double-decker, the Metrobus, with the economical Gardner 6LXB as the standard engine. It also had hydraulic brakes, which LT favoured over air brakes, and a Voith automatic gearbox incorporating a retarder. Production started in 1978, with LT taking five for evaluation and then ordering large batches to build up a fleet of 1,440 by 1986. In addition three Metrobus IIs were ordered as part of the Alternative Vehicle Evaluation. The Metrobus II had been introduced in 1982 and had a simpler and lighter structure than the original. In the end only two were delivered, as M1441/2 in 1984, one with a Cummins engine, the other a Gardner. The third would have been M1443 with changes that merited the designation Metrobus III. Engine options being considered for M1443 were an air-cooled Deutz or Gardner's five-cylinder 5LXCT.

The Metrobus IIs were followed in 1987-88 by 14 second-hand Metrobuses for services in the Potters Bar area, including two with bodies by Alexander of Falkirk. Finally 29 Mark II models were added to the fleet in 1987-88 for the Harrow Buses operation. While most of LT's Metrobuses had Gardner engines, Cummins L10s were fitted to 23 vehicles. The 1988 Metrobuses were the last new Gardner-engined buses for London Buses.

MCW also produced a 12m-long double-deck express coach, the Metroliner, developed from a three-axle Metrobus chassis designed for operation in Hong Kong. LT purchased four in 1986 for the London Liner service to Birmingham, operated jointly with West Midlands Travel. The Metroliners had 290bhp Cummins L10 engines. The service only lasted for around 12 months and all four Metroliners were then sold.

At the 1986 Motor Show MCW launched an integral midibus, the Metrorider, which was an attractive little 25-seater just under 7m long. MCW's aim was to produce a more durable product than the van-derived minibuses then in vogue. In its launch announcement MCW said the Metrorider would be "more durable and require less frequent maintenance attention in order to optimise the financial equation of this class of vehicle operation". London Buses specified the six-cylinder 115bhp Cummins B-series engine and an Allison automatic gearbox, and in 1987-88 built up a fleet of 134, with most of the later vehicles being bigger, 8.4m long, models.

However MCW was in trouble, a victim of the downturn in bus orders following the 1986 deregulation of local bus services outside London. The company closed in 1989 and the rights to the Metrorider design were purchased by Optare of Leeds. A considerably improved model – now known as the MetroRider with a capital R in the middle – was launched in 1989. Improvements to the Metrorider were badly needed, so much so that shortly before MCW's collapse a group of disgruntled operators formed a Metrorider User Group to lobby the manufacturer. Insufficient development work by MCW meant that a variety of faults were appearing, including structural failures.

London Buses bought 107 Optare MetroRiders between 1990 and 1993. These were numbered in series with the MCW buses and are included here. They were London Buses' last new front-engined midibuses; the rear-engined Dennis Dart was the new shape in small buses. A part-built MetroRider was supplied by Optare for display at the London Transport Museum and carried fleet number MRL242 at the end of the MetroRider series. It moved to the London Bus Museum at Brooklands in 2017.

Specifications

Model	Engine	Displacement	Power output	Gearbox
Metro-Scania	Scania D11	11 litres	170bhp	Scania automatic
Metropolitan	Scania D11	11 litres	170bhp	Scania automatic
Metrobus	Gardner 6LXB	10.45 litres	170bhp	Voith D851 automatic
Metroliner	Cummins L10	10 litres	290bhp	Voith D854 automatic
Metrorider/MetroRider	Cummins 6B	5.9 litres	115bhp	Allison AT545 automatic

- Cummins L10 engines were fitted to M1084-1105, 1442.

MS1-6	PGC 201-206L	Metro-Scania CR111MH	MCW B37+29D	1973
MD1-83	KJD 201-283P	MCW Metropolitan	MCW H43/29D	1976
MD84-164	OUC 84-164R	MCW Metropolitan	MCW H43/29D	1976-77
MT1-3	THX 101-103S	MCW Metrobus	MCW H43/28D	1978

- MT1-3 were renumbered M1-3 before entering service.

M1-5	THX 101-105S	MCW Metrobus	MCW H43/28D	1978
M6-95	WYW 6-95T	MCW Metrobus	MCW H43/24D	1978-79
M96-205	BYX 96-205V	MCW Metrobus	MCW H43/24D	1979
M206-315	BYX 206-315V	MCW Metrobus	MCW H43/28D	1980
M316-345	EYE 316-345V	MCW Metrobus	MCW H43/28D	1980
M346-430	GYE 346-430W	MCW Metrobus	MCW H43/28D	1980
M431-446	GYE 431-446W	MCW Metrobus	MCW H43/9D	1980

Harrow Buses used this attractive livery when the operation was launched in 1987 to run LRT tendered services in the Harrow area. Its fleet included 29 Mark II Metrobuses which were leased from Plaxton Coach Sales. M1480 is in Edgware. Tony Wilson

M447-605	GYE 447-605W	MCW Metrobus	MCW H43/28D	1980-81
M606-631	KYO 606-631X	MCW Metrobus	MCW H43/28D	1981
M632-805	KYV 632-805X	MCW Metrobus	MCW H43/28D	1981-82
M806-891	OJD 806-891Y	MCW Metrobus	MCW H43/28D	1983
M892-955	A892-955 SUL	MCW Metrobus	MCW H43/28D	1983
M956-999	A956-999 SYF	MCW Metrobus	MCW H43/28D	1984
M1000-1005	A700-705 THV	MCW Metrobus	MCW H43/28D	1984
M1006-1029	A706-729 THV	MCW Metrobus	MCW H43/9DL	1984
M1030-1055	A730-755 THV	MCW Metrobus	MCW H43/28D	1984
M1056-1305	B56-305 WUL	MCW Metrobus	MCW H43/28D	1984-85
M1306-1440	C306-440 BUV	MCW Metrobus	MCW H43/28D	1985-86
M1441-1442	A441-442 UUV	MCW Metrobus II	MCW H43/28D	1984
M1443	GBU 1V	MCW Metrobus	MCW H43/30F	1979
M1444-1445	GBU 4-5V	MCW Metrobus	MCW H43/30F	1979
M1446-1447	GBU 8-9V	MCW Metrobus	MCW H43/30F	1979
M1448-1449	UWW 518-519X	MCW Metrobus	Alexander R H43/32F	1982
M1450-1451	CUB 539-540Y	MCW Metrobus II	MCW H46/30F	1983
M1452-1478	E452-478 SON	MCW Metrobus II	MCW H45/30F	1987-88
M1479-1480	E479-480 UOF	MCW Metrobus II	MCW H45/30F	1988
M1481-1485	VRG 415-419T	MCW Metrobus	MCW H46/30F	1979

- M431-446 and M1006-1029 had large luggage racks in the lower saloon and were used on Airbus services from central London to Heathrow Airport.
- M1000-1055 were to have been registered A500-555 SYL
- M1441/2 were part of the Alternative Vehicle Evaluation programme at Stockwell garage.
- The number M1443 was originally intended for a Metrobus III with registration A443 UUV, changed to B443 WUC when it appeared the bus would be delivered later than planned. In the event it wasn't built.
- M1443-1447 ex Greater Manchester PTE, 1987.
- M1448-1451 ex West Yorkshire PTE, 1987.
- M1452-1480 were operated by Harrow Buses and were leased from Plaxton Coach Sales.
- M1479-1480 were diverted from an East Kent order.
- M1481-1485 ex Busways Travel Services, 1988.

Four MCW Metroliners were bought in 1986 for a new London Coaches service to Birmingham. This was operated jointly with West Midlands Travel which had three identical coaches in overall blue. The Metroliners were London's first three-axle double-deck motorbuses since AEC Renowns of the 1930s. *Tony Wilson*

A London Buses poster for its Birmingham coach service featured a touch of humour.

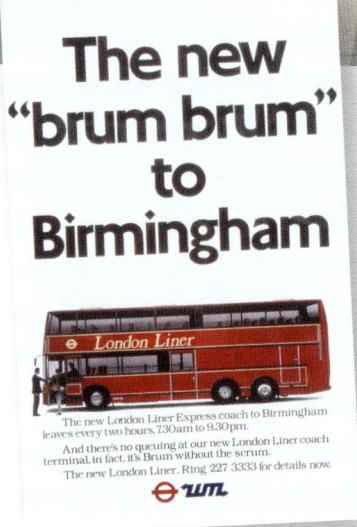

The new "brum brum" to Birmingham

The new London Liner Express coach to Birmingham leaves every two hours, 7.30am to 9.30pm.
And there's no queuing at our new London Liner coach terminal, in fact, it's Brum without the scrum.
The new London Liner. Ring 227 3333 for details now.

ML1-4	C101-104 DYE	MCW Metroliner	MCW CH53/16DT	1986
MR1-18	D461-478 PON	MCW Metrorider	MCW B23F	1987
MR19-22	D479-482 PON	MCW Metrorider	MCW DP25F	1987
MR23-52	E123-152 KYW	MCW Metrorider	MCW B25F	1987
MR53-54	E929-930 KYR	MCW Metrorider	MCW B23F	1987
MR55-64	E631-640 KYW	MCW Metrorider	MCW B23F	1987
MRL65-74	E641-650 KYW	MCW Metrorider	MCW B30F	1988
MRL75-76	E705-706 LYU	MCW Metrorider	MCW DP33F	1988
MRL77	F197 YDA	MCW Metrorider	MCW B28F	1988
MRL78-92	F182-196 YDA	MCW Metrorider	MCW DP28F	1988
MR93-94	E873-874 NJD	MCW Metrorider	MCW DP25F	1988
MR95-98	F895-898 OYR	MCW Metrorider	MCW DP25F	1988
MR99-105	F99-105 YVP	MCW Metrorider	MCW DP23F	1988
MRL106-133	F106-133 YVP	MCW Metrorider	MCW B28F	1988
MR134	D482 NOX	MCW Metrorider	MCW B25F	1986
MRL135	H135 TGO	Optare MetroRider	Optare B28F	1990
MRL136-159	H136-159 UUA	Optare MetroRider	Optare B26F	1990-91
MRL160-163	H160-163 WWT	Optare MetroRider	Optare B26F	1991

MRL164	H564 WWR	Optare MetroRider	Optare B26F	1991
MRL165-176	H165-176 WWT	Optare MetroRider	Optare B26F	1991
MRL177-190	H677-690 YGO	Optare MetroRider	Optare B26F	1991
MRL191-199	J691-699 CGK	Optare MetroRider	Optare B26F	1991
MRL200	J710 CGK	Optare MetroRider	Optare B26F	1991
MRL201-209	J701-709 CGK	Optare MetroRider	Optare B26F	1991
MRL210-221	J210-221 BWU	Optare MetroRider	Optare B26F	1991-92
MRL222	K422 HWY	Optare MetroRider	Optare B26F	1993
MRL223	K223 MGT	Optare MetroRider	Optare B26F	1993
MRL224-241	K424-441 HWY	Optare MetroRider	Optare B26F	1993

MRL242 allocated to a part-built MetroRider which was an exhibit at the London Transport Museum.

- MR53-64 were new to Bexleybus where they were numbered 29-40.
- MR93-98 were briefly numbered SG1-6 when new.
- MR134 ex MCW demonstrator, 1988.
- MR1-22, MRL77-92, MR99-105, MRL106-133, MR134 were registered in Birmingham by MCW.
- MRL136-176, 210-222, 224-241 were registered in Leeds by Optare.

SG1-2	E873-874 NJD	MCW Metrorider	MCW DP25F	1988
SG3-6	F895-898 OYR	MCW Metrorider	MCW DP25F	1988

- SG1-6 were operated in conjunction with Wandsworth Health Authority on services to St George's Hospital, hence the SG classification. They were renumbered MR93-98 soon after entering service.

The MCW Metrorider was a neat little vehicle which differed from its midibus contemporaries in being a purpose-designed bus built by a specialist bus manufacturer. London United MR16 was a 23-seater which had been new in 1987 to Westlink. This is a 1990 view in Hanworth. Tony Wilson

Leyland Titan and Olympian

Despite having placed the single biggest bus order in Daimler's history, for 1,600 chassis, London Transport had quickly decided it didn't really like the Daimler Fleetline. It wanted a bus designed to meet its specific needs. Leyland obliged with project B15, a totally new integral double-decker which was launched as the Titan in 1977. Key features included independent front suspension, hydraulic brakes (an LT requirement which was out of step with the air brakes used by the rest of the industry), an automatic gearbox incorporating a retarder, and engine encapsulation to reduce noise. Unusually deep lower deck windows made the interior bright and airy, and gave standing passengers a better view out of the bus. The interior layout was developed after trials of what

The Titan was designed by Leyland to meet London's requirements and was an advanced model for its time featuring integral construction, hydraulic brakes and a gearbox with an integral retarder. T7 shows the livery applied to the first 31 Titans; subsequent deliveries were all-over red. The advert on the side is for Amphora pipe tobacco, surely a minority interest among smokers by 1979.

A cutaway drawing produced by Leyland shows the layout of the Titan, including the unusual location of the radiator mounted high above the engine compartment on the offside of the bus.

Leyland called human factors engineering, an ergonomic study of how people moved around inside buses.

In a 1976 brochure promoting the B15 ("designed to win people back to buses") Leyland took the unusual step of criticising the industry to which it was trying to sell buses, providing ammunition for those who claimed the company had a high-handed attitude towards its customers. The opening paragraph set the tone: "Remember the old days of bus travel? They were, to put it bluntly, desperately bad. Poorly ventilated, ill-lit, inadequately heated with an upper deck resembling the proverbial smoker's den, buses over the years have inflicted a great deal of daily misery on the travelling public. Small wonder that people took to the private car, not just in their thousands but quite literally in their millions." And, one might reasonably ask of Leyland's copywriter, who built many of these buses?

Then there was the condescending hyperbole about the B15's low noise: "Rather than bore you with details about decibel levels, we'd like to draw a straight comparison. Remember those lovely quiet electric trolleybuses? B15 is at that level inside and out. And for those of you who don't remember so far back, B15 is even quieter than some modern cars." B15 as quiet as a trolleybus? Where's the Advertising Standards Authority when you need it?

After evaluating two B15 prototypes in 1976 and 1978 LT ordered 250 for delivery in 1978-79, and a further 250 for 1979-80. But that didn't happen. Labour problems at Park Royal which was building the Titan saw the factory close in 1980 with Titan production being moved some 300 miles north to the Leyland National factory in Workington. Instead of having 500 Titans in service in 1980, it would be 1982 before that number was reached. LT cancelled 100 of its Titans, and ordered more MCW Metrobuses to compensate. Once production got underway at Workington further orders were placed and by 1984 there were 1,125 in London service.

The Titan had failed to meet Leyland's expectations – in 1974 it was forecasting that it would be building 1,500 a year by 1978. In reality, *total* production was just 1,158. Market forecasting never was a very exact science. LT had emerged as the only significant buyer and when it concluded in 1983 that it would stop buying Titans because they were more expensive to operate than Metrobuses that spelled the end of the Titan. Most of those for London had Gardner 6LXB engines, but ten had Leyland engines.

Generally Titans were based in garages east of an imaginary north-south line through Charing Cross, while Metrobuses were allocated to garages west of the line.

Leyland had in fact quickly realised that the integral Titan was not the bus most of its customers wanted, and added the Olympian to its model range in 1980, using much the same drivetrain as the Titan but in a chassis with a perimeter frame and a beam axle at the front. London tried three with Eastern Coach Works bodies in 1984 as part of its Alternative Vehicle Evaluation, and then ordered 260, also bodied by ECW, for delivery in 1986-87.

For the new Bexleybus operation in 1987 London Buses took 28 Gardner-engined Olympians which were diverted from the Greater Manchester PTE and were built to the PTE's specification with single-door Northern Counties bodies. Further orders were placed for 23 with Leyland bodies in 1989, and 40 with Alexander bodies in 1992. These 63 buses had Cummins L10 engines. Olympian L354 was the last new Leyland for London Buses.

Unusual Olympians in 1986 were two long-wheelbase models with TL11 engines and East Lancs coach bodies. These were in London Coaches livery and were for a short-lived London Liner express service to Eastbourne, operated jointly with Eastbourne Borough Transport. Both were sold in 1990.

The chassis for Olympians L1-263 and L315-354 were built at Workington; the others were produced at the Farington factory in the town of Leyland.

Specifications

Model	Engine	Displacement	Power output	Gearbox
TNLXB	Gardner 6LXB	10.45 litres	170bhp	Leyland Hydracyclic
TNL11	Leyland L11	11.1 litres	170bhp	Leyland Hydracyclic
TNTL11	Leyland TL11	11.1 litres	170bhp	Leyland Hydracyclic
ONLXB/1R	Gardner 6LXB	10.45 litres	170bhp	Voith D851
ONLXB/1RH	Gardner 6LXB	10.45 litres	170bhp	Leyland Hydracyclic
ONTL11/1R	Leyland TL11	11.1 litres	170bhp	Leyland Hydracyclic
ONTL11/2RHSp	Leyland TL11	11.1 litres	245bhp	Leyland Hydracyclic
ONCL10	Cummins L10	10 litres	180bhp	ZF automatic
ON2R50C13Z4	Cummins L10	10 litres	180bhp	ZF automatic

T1-2	THX 401-402S	Leyland Titan TNLXB2RRSp	Park Royal H44/22D	1978
T3-67	WYV 3-67T	Leyland Titan TNLXB2RRSp	Park Royal H44/22D	1978-79
T68-70	CUL 68-70V	Leyland Titan TNLXB2RRSp	Park Royal H44/22D	1979
T71-225	CUL 71-225V	Leyland Titan TNLXB2RRSp	Park Royal H44/24D	1979-80
T226-250	EYE 226-250V	Leyland Titan TNLXB2RRSp	Park Royal H44/24D	1980
T251-260	GYE 251-260W	Leyland Titan TNLXB2RR	Park Royal H44/24D	1981
T261	GYE 261W	Leyland Titan TNTL112RR	Park Royal H44/24D	1981
T262-263	GYE 262-263W	Leyland Titan TNLXB2RR	Park Royal H44/24D	1981
T264-281	GYE 264-281W	Leyland Titan TNLXB2RR	Leyland H44/24D	1981
T282-310	KYN 282-310X	Leyland Titan TNLXB2RR	Leyland H44/24D	1981
T311-344	KYV 311-344X	Leyland Titan TNLXB2RR	Leyland H44/24D	1982
T345	KYV 345X	Leyland Titan TNL112RR	Leyland H44/24D	1982
T346-549	KYV 346-549X	Leyland Titan TNLXB2RR	Leyland H44/24D	1982
T550-675	NUW 550-675Y	Leyland Titan TNLXB2RR	Leyland H44/24D	1982
T676-797	OHV 676-797Y	Leyland Titan TNLXB2RR	Leyland H44/24D	1982-83
T798-815	OHV 798-815Y	Leyland Titan TNLXB2RR	Leyland H44/26D	1983
T816-822	RYK 816-822Y	Leyland Titan TNLXB2RR	Leyland H44/26D	1983
T823-875	A823-875 SUL	Leyland Titan TNLXB2RR	Leyland H44/26D	1983

T876-880	A876-880 SUL	Leyland Titan TNTL112RR	Leyland H44/26D	1983
T881-885	A881-885 SUL	Leyland Titan TNL112RR	Leyland H44/26D	1983
T886-999	A886-999 SYE	Leyland Titan TNLXB2RR	Leyland H44/26D	1983
T1000-1055	A600-655 THV	Leyland Titan TNLXB2RR	Leyland H44/26D	1984
T1056-1078	A56-78 THX	Leyland Titan TNLXB2RR	Leyland H44/26D	1984
T1079-1125	B79-125 WUV	Leyland Titan TNLXB2RR	Leyland H44/26D	1984
T1126-1130	WDA 1-5T	Leyland Titan TNLXB1RF	Park Royal H47/26F	1978-79
T1131	BCK 706R	Leyland B15.05	Park Royal H44/23F	1977

- T1126-30 ex West Midlands PTE, 1984.
- T1131 ex Fishwick, Leyland in 1987; it had originally been a Leyland demonstrator in London in 1977-78.

London Buses' last big double-deck order was for 260 Leyland Olympians with ECW bodies. When new they were all-over red with yellow entrance doors as illustrated by L25 in Sidcup in the summer of 1986. The split-level entrance step was designed to improve access for people with restricted mobility. *Tony Wilson*

L1	A101 SYE	Leyland Olympian ONTL11/1R	ECW H47/28D	1984
L2-3	A102-103 SYE	Leyland Olympian ONLXB/1R	ECW H47/28D	1984
L4-20	C804-820 BYY	Leyland Olympian ONLXB/1RH	ECW H42/26D	1986
L21-122	C21-122 CHM	Leyland Olympian ONLXB/1RH	ECW H42/26D	1986
L123-166	D123-166 FYM	Leyland Olympian ONLXB/1RH	ECW H42/26D	1986
L167-171	D167-171 FYM	Leyland Olympian ONLXB/1RH	ECW CH42/26D	1986
L172-259	D172-259 FYM	Leyland Olympian ONLXB/1RH	ECW H42/26D	1986-87
L260	D260 FYM	Leyland Olympian ONLXB/1RH	ECW CH42/26D	1987
L261-263	D261-263 FUL	Leyland Olympian ONLXB/1RH	ECW CH42/26D	1987
L264-291	E901-928 KYR	Leyland Olympian ONLXB/1RH	Northern Counties Palatine H43/30F	1987
L292-306	G292-306 UYK	Leyland Olympian ONCL10/1RZ	Leyland H47/31F	1989
L307-311	G307-311 UYK	Leyland Olympian ON2R50C13Z4	Leyland H47/31F	1989
L312-314	G312-314 UYK	Leyland Olympian ON2R50C13Z4	Leyland CH47/31F	1989
L315-332	J315-332 BSH	Leyland Olympian ON2R50C13Z4	Alexander R H43/25D	1992
L333	J433 BSH	Leyland Olympian ON2R50C13Z4	Alexander R H43/25D	1992
L334-354	J334-354 BSH	Leyland Olympian ON2R50C13Z4	Alexander R H43/25D	1992

- L1-3 were part of the Alternative Vehicle Evaluation programme at Stockwell garage.
- L264-291 were new to Bexleybus where they were numbered 1-28. They were diverted from Greater Manchester PTE and were on lease from Plaxton Coach Sales.
- L292-314 were new to London United and carried Riverside Bus branding.
- L315-354 were new to Leaside.

LC1-2	C201-202 DYE	Leyland Olympian ONTL11/2RHSpEast Lancs CH49/21FT	1986

- These were operated by London Coaches.

Bexleybus used this smart livery which gave no clue that the operation was in any way connected with London Buses. Officially this Leyland Olympian was L278 in the London Buses fleet, but the only fleet number on display is its Bexleybus identity, 15. *Peter Rowlands*

LEYLAND TITAN AND OLYMPIAN 99

Forty Olympians with Cummins engines and single-door Alexander bodies were London Buses' last new Leylands. They entered service in 1992. All were allocated to Leaside, initially at Stamford Hill garage. The last four had high-backed seats in the lower saloon and large gold fleetnames on the upper deck side panels. L351 is on a railway replacement service in Pinner in the spring of 1994. *Keith Grimes*

The two long-wheelbase Olympian coaches had East Lancs bodies and Leyland engines. They were striking vehicles, but the express service to Eastbourne for which they were bought was not a success and they were sold when they were just four years old. LC2 is in London Coaches' Wandsworth garage. *Tony Wilson*

Leyland Lynx

The Lynx was introduced by Leyland in 1986 to replace the National and was produced at the former National factory in Workington. Unlike the National, the Lynx featured a separate chassis which was to be made available to other bodybuilders, although all of the Lynxes sold in Britain were fitted with Leyland's own square-styled body.

Two Cummins-engined examples joined the London Buses fleet in 1988. LX1 and LX2 were operated on behalf of the London Borough of Hillingdon and were in a red and yellow livery for route 128, Ruislip to Harefield Hospital. They were followed in 1989 by LX3-8 which also had Cummins engines and were bought for use by London United on service 283, East Acton to West Brompton.

Finally, in 1989 Hillingdon bought three second-hand Lynxes, LX9-11, which had been new in 1987 to Merthyr Tydfil Transport and these, too, were in route 128 colours. Unlike the other London Buses Lynxes they had Leyland engines. The Hillingdon Lynxes were bought by London Buses in 1991.

Specifications

	Model	Engine	Displacement	Power output	Gearbox
LX1-2	LX112L10ZR1R	Cummins L10	10 litres	210bhp	ZF 4HP500 automatic
LX3-8	LX2R11C15Z4S	Cummins L10	10 litres	210bhp	ZF 4HP500 automatic
LX9-11	LX112TL11ZR1R	Leyland TL11H	11 litres	210bhp	ZF 4HP500 automatic

LX1-2	F101-102 GRM	Leyland Lynx	Leyland B47F	1988
LX3-8	G73-78 UYV	Leyland Lynx	Leyland B47F	1989
LX9-10	D105-106 NDW	Leyland Lynx	Leyland B51F	1987
LX11	D111 NDW	Leyland Lynx	Leyland B51F	1987

- LX1-2 were registered by Leyland Bus in Carlisle, the nearest licensing office to Leyland's Workington factory.
- LX9-11 ex Merthyr Tydfil Transport, 1989. They were quickly re-registered 809-811 DYE, numbers transferred from Routemasters RM1809-1811.

LT's first two Leyland Lynxes were operated on behalf of the London Borough of Hillingdon and were in this dedicated livery for route 128. LX1 is at Ruislip station. This livery was also applied to the three ex-Merthyr Tydfil Lynxes. *Tony Wilson*

Mercedes-Benz

Here's a measure of the changes taking place in London. In 1968 LT was taking delivery of the last of 2,760 Routemasters. In 1978 it was receiving the last of 2,646 DMS-class Fleetlines. And in 1988 its successor, London Buses, was buying buses based on German-built light truck chassis.

The Mercedes-Benz T2 range of commercial vehicles was launched in 1986 and quickly proved a popular choice with bus operators in deregulated Britain. The two most common models for bus use were the 709D and the 811D chassis cowls. The chassis designations gave a rough indication of the gross vehicle weight, nominally 7 tonnes (actually 6.6) for the 709D and 8 tonnes (actually 7.5) for the 811D, and of the power output, 88bhp on the lighter model and 114bhp on the heavier one. Both were powered by Mercedes' four-cylinder 3.64-litre engine which was naturally-aspirated in the 709D and turbocharged on the 811D. They had disc brakes on the front wheels and Mercedes four-speed automatic gearboxes.

The Mercedes-Benz/Reeve Burgess combination was popular throughout Britain, but there were only 13 in the London Buses fleet. Southall Shuttle MT8 featured on the cover of a Mercedes-Benz brochure for the manufacturer's UK minibus and midibus models.

A CentreWest recruitment leaflet for Gold Arrow drivers (average earnings of £195 a week in 1988) illustrated an Alexander-bodied Mercedes-Benz which, the leaflet promised, was "smooth and easy to drive". The doors on the MA-class Mercedes were wide, but not as wide as this drawing suggests. The Gold Arrow routes, on which the Mercedes replaced Routemasters, were the 28, Golders Green to Wandsworth, and 31, Camden Town to Chelsea.

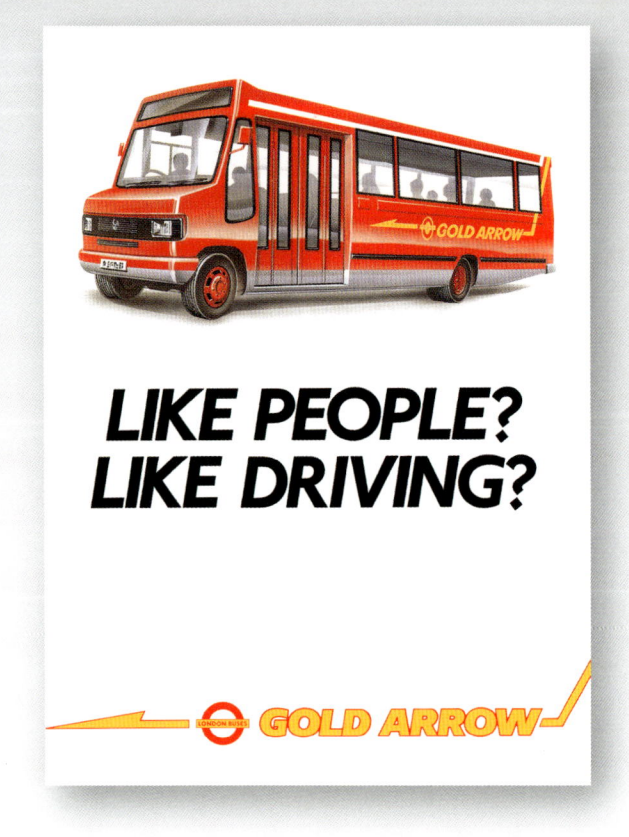

LIKE PEOPLE? LIKE DRIVING?

GOLD ARROW

London Buses took 312 Mercedes between 1988 and 1993, most of them the heavier 811D. The main bodywork suppliers were Alexander (134) and Optare (123), with smaller numbers coming from Wright (37), Reeve Burgess (13) and Carlyle (five). The Optare bodies were StarRiders, which dispensed with the standard Mercedes-Benz bonnet assembly to give a smoother front profile, sometimes referred to as a fast front. A similarly-styled front was used by Wright on one of the MW-class buses. The StarRiders also had wider entrances – described as fast flow – than previous midibuses, and set the pattern for subsequent deliveries by other builders. The Mercedes midibuses operated by London Buses were generally around 8.4m (27ft 6in) long.

Specifications

Model	Engine	Displacement	Power output
709D	Mercedes OM364	3.64 litres	88bhp
811D	Mercedes OM364A	3.64 litres	114bhp

MA1-45	F601-645 XMS	Mercedes-Benz 811D	Alexander AM B28F	1988-89
MA46-55	F946-955 BMS	Mercedes-Benz 811D	Alexander AM B28F	1989
MA56-100	F656-700 XMS	Mercedes-Benz 811D	Alexander AM B28F	1989
MA101-107	F701-707 XMS	Mercedes-Benz 811D	Alexander AM DP28F	1989
MA108-124	G108-124 PGT	Mercedes-Benz 811D	Alexander AM B28F	1990
MA125-134	H425-434 XGK	Mercedes-Benz 811D	Alexander AM B28F	1991

- F690-699 XMS were delivered as MA51-55, 46-50; before entering service they were renumbered MA90-99 to match their registrations. Consequently the buses which were to have been MA90-99 became instead MA46-55 with new F-BMS registrations.
- MA1-107 were new to CentreWest for Gold Arrow and U-Line services and were registered in Stirling by Alexander.
- MA108-134 were new to London General and carried Streetline branding.

And here's a real MA. Alexander was London Buses' biggest supplier of bodies on Mercedes-Benz chassis, most of them going to CentreWest. MA106 was new in 1989 and is parked outside Uxbridge garage. *J Birkett*

| MC1 | F430 BOP | Mercedes-Benz 811D | Carlyle C17 B28F | 1989 |
| MC2-5 | H882-885 LOX | Mercedes-Benz 811D | Carlyle C17 B28F | 1990 |

- MC1 ex Carlyle demonstrator, 1990.
- These buses were operated by Selkent and carried Roundabout branding. They were registered in Birmingham by Carlyle.

MT1-5	F391-395 DHL	Mercedes-Benz 709D	Reeve Burgess Beaver B20FL	1988
MT6	F396 DHL	Mercedes-Benz 811D	Reeve Burgess Beaver C33F	1988
MT7-8	G537-538 GBD	Mercedes-Benz 709D	Reeve Burgess Beaver B20FL	1989

- MT1-5, 7-8 were for the Southall Shuttle, part-funded by the London Borough of Ealing. MT1-5 were registered in Sheffield by Reeve Burgess. MT7-8 were registered in Northampton by Mercedes-Benz.
- MT6 was renumbered MTL6 in 1991. It had a single-piece door (the other Beavers had two-piece doors) and was unusual in being fitted with dual controls for driver training, with the instructor sitting in the courier seat. It was allocated to Selkent and registered in Sheffield by Reeve Burgess which was based in Pilsley, Derbyshire.

MTL1	G621 XLO	Mercedes-Benz 811D	Reeve Burgess Beaver B26F	1989
MTL2	G222 KWE	Mercedes-Benz 811D	Reeve Burgess Beaver B26F	1989
MTL3	H189 RWF	Mercedes-Benz 811D	Reeve Burgess Beaver B26F	1989
MTL4-5	H191-192 RWF	Mercedes-Benz 811D	Reeve Burgess Beaver B26F	1989
MTL6	VLT 77	Mercedes-Benz 811D	Reeve Burgess Beaver C33F	1988

- MTL2-5 were registered in Sheffield by Reeve Burgess.
- MTL6 was previously numbered MT6 and was originally registered F396 DHL.

MW1-16	HDZ 2601-2616	Mercedes-Benz 811D	Wright Nimbus B26F	1989
MW17	LDZ 9017	Mercedes-Benz 811D	Wright Nimbus B26F	1992
MW18-37	NDZ 7918-7937	Mercedes-Benz 811D	Wright Nimbus B26F	1993

- MW1-16 were new to Selkent.
- MW17 had a Wright-designed fast front in place of the standard Mercedes bonnet.
- MW18-37 were new to London Northern.
- All of the MWs were registered in Ballymena by Wright.

The Optare StarRider was probably the most successful attempt by a UK coachbuilder to disguise the light truck origins of its small bus. Optare tended not to display chassis makers' badges, but the Mercedes-Benz three-pointed star was fitted to the StarRider. The Mercedes badge would resonate with bus passengers in a way which the DAF name on the Delta and Spectra would not. London Buses had 126 StarRiders; East London SR41 of 1989 is in Shadwell on route 100 to Liverpool Street Station. *Tony Wilson*

There were 37 Wright-bodied Mercedes-Benz 811Ds. London Northern Midilink MW20 is at Potters Bar. The main section of the 326 ran between New Barnet and Brent Cross. The route had been started in 1991 using Optare StarRiders; these were replaced by new MW-class Mercedes in 1993. *Tony Wilson*

SR1-4	E711-714 LYU	Mercedes-Benz 811D	Optare StarRider B26F	1988
SR5-28	F905-928 YWY	Mercedes-Benz 811D	Optare StarRider B26F	1988
SR29-53	F29-53 CWY	Mercedes-Benz 811D	Optare StarRider B26F	1989
SR54-59	F154-159 FWY	Mercedes-Benz 811D	Optare StarRider B26F	1989
SR60-81	F160-181 FWY	Mercedes-Benz 811D	Optare StarRider B26F	1989
SR82-121	G82-121 KUB	Mercedes-Benz 811D	Optare StarRider B26F	1989
SR122-123	G122-123 SMV	Mercedes-Benz 811D	Optare StarRider B26F	1990

- SR54-59 were in Bexleybus cream and blue livery with fleet numbers 108-113.
- SR5-121 were registered in Leeds by Optare.

Renault

The Dodge S56 was part of a range of light truck chassis launched in the UK by Chrysler in 1979 and built in Dunstable. The operation was taken over by Renault in 1981. London's first S-series models were two S56s bought in 1983 for Potters Bar local service PB1, where they replaced 16-seat Ford Transits. They had six-cylinder Perkins engines.

From the mid 1980s Renault offered the heavier S75 with a gross vehicle weight of 7.5 tonnes and powered by a four-cylinder turbocharged Perkins Phaser engine. Those for London had Allison automatic gearboxes. The S75 was a competitor for the Mercedes-Benz 811D but never achieved the same level of popularity. London Buses had 312 Mercedes midibuses

LT bought two 19-seat Dodge S56s in 1983 to provide extra capacity on Potters Bar local service PB1. The utilitarian-looking body was built in Maidstone by Rootes. The Dodges ran on the PB1 until 1986. *Tony Wilson*

Renault, like Mercedes-Benz, was keen to promote its success in London, and this 1990 sales leaflet illustrated one of the 33 S75s with Reeve Burgess bodies which were delivered to East London. Note the wide doorway, popularly described as a fast-flow entrance. It was specified on many of London's small buses but was rare elsewhere. The silver oval is Renault's "Seal of Approval" for Reeve Burgess bodies.

compared with 125 Renaults plus the two early Dodges. The RB-class Renaults operated in East London, while the 90 RW-class vehicles – at that time both Wright's and Renault's biggest single British bus orders – were at CentreWest for E-line services in Ealing and for the Hanwell Hoppa. All 35 RB-class buses were sold to the Yorkshire Traction Group in 1994-95.

In addition to the 125 midibuses taken into the London Buses fleet in 1990-91, there was one full-size Renault, a PR100. This was a design introduced in 1971 by Berliet, which was taken over by Renault in 1975. Northern Counties of Wigan reached an agreement with Renault to sell the PR100 in the UK, but with little success: only five were built. Part of the problem was that the PR100 was an 18-year-old design, and it had already been replaced in France by the R312. RN1 was initially operated by East London. It was sold to Parfitts of Rhymney Bridge in 1993.

Specifications

Model	Engine	Displacement	Power output
S56C	Perkins	4.05 litres	94bhp
S75	Perkins Phaser 110T	3.99 litres	109bhp
PR100.2	Renault MIPS 06.20.45	9.8 litres	196bhp

A1-2	NYN 1-2Y	Dodge S56C	Rootes B19F	1983
RB1-25	G871-895 WML	Renault S75	Reeve Burgess Beaver B29F	1990
RB26-33	H126-133 AML	Renault S75	Reeve Burgess Beaver B29F	1990
RB34	J134 HME	Renault S75	Reeve Burgess Beaver B29F	1991
RB35	J235 LLK	Renault S75	Reeve Burgess Beaver B29F	1991

- RB34-35 were on loan from Renault in 1991-92.

RW1-90	HDZ 5401-5490	Renault S75	Wright Nimbus B28F	1990
RN1	G276 VML	Renault PR100.2	Northern Counties B51+24F	1989

RENAULT **107**

The marriage of the sophisticated Alusuisse construction system used by Wright with a modified truck chassis built by Renault seemed an odd match. CentreWest had 90 Nimbus bodies on S75 chassis. RW5 is in Northwood Hills in 1991 on route 282, Mount Vernon Hospital to Ealing Hospital, where the Renaults had replaced Metrobuses in the previous year. *Tony Wilson*

The PR100 was a classic French urban bus design of the 1970s. Renault and Northern Counties teamed up, unsuccessfully as it turned out, to sell it in the UK in the late 1980s. London Buses took one for evaluation. Dot matrix destination displays were briefly popular in Britain but were rare in London. *Tony Wilson*

Iveco

Iveco, the Industrial Vehicles Corporation, was an amalgamation in 1975 of five European truck and bus manufacturers – Fiat, OM, Lancia, Unic and Magirus Deutz. The Iveco Daily light truck chassis, launched in 1978, was used as the basis of a small bus by a number of British operators from the mid 1980s. The Daily was powered by a 2.45-litre Iveco engine. The 1986 buses had the original angular Daily bonnet; the later vehicles had a more rounded style introduced in 1989.

The 24 RH-class Ivecos were the only London buses to be bodied by Robin Hood Vehicle Builders which despite its name was based not in Nottingham but in Fareham, Hampshire, and was run by a Mr Robin Hood. The FM-class buses were the first Marshall bodies for London since 125 AEC Swifts delivered in 1970-71.

As well as supplying midibuses to London, Iveco provided 8.1-litre 8361 engines which were used to re-power 201 Fleetlines and 150 Routemasters in the late 1980s and early 1990s.

Specifications

Model	Engine	Displacement	Power output
RH	Iveco 8140	2.45 litres	92bhp
FM/FR	Iveco 8140	2.45 litres	103bhp

FM1-10	K521-530 EFL	Iveco Daily 49.10	Marshall C29 B23F	1993

- FM1-10 were for Roundabout services in the Orpington area. They were registered in Peterborough by Marshall.

FR1-8	H701-708 YUV	Iveco Daily 49.10	Reeve Burgess Beaver B20FL	1990

- FR1-8 were operated by London United on a service which was supported by the London Borough of Hounslow.

RH1-12	C501-512 DYM	Iveco Daily 49.10	Robin Hood City Nippy B21F	1986
RH13-14	D513-514 FYL	Iveco Daily 49.10	Robin Hood City Nippy B21F	1986
RH15-18	C515-518 DYM	Iveco Daily 49.10	Robin Hood City Nippy B21F	1986
RH19-20	D519-520 FYL	Iveco Daily 49.10	Robin Hood City Nippy B21F	1986
RH21	C521 DYM	Iveco Daily 49.10	Robin Hood City Nippy B21F	1986
RH22	D522 FYL	Iveco Daily 49.10	Robin Hood City Nippy B21F	1986
RH23	C523 DYM	Iveco Daily 49.10	Robin Hood City Nippy DP21F	1986
RH24	D524 FYL	Iveco Daily 49.10	Robin Hood City Nippy DP21F	1986

- RH1-24 were new to Orpington Buses in maroon and grey Roundabout livery and were to have been registered C501-524 DYM. Thirteen were repainted blue and cream and transferred to Bexleybus for the start of operations in January 1988.

London Buses had 42 Iveco Daily minibuses. The most numerous type was the 24-strong RH class with Robin Hood bodies bought for the Roundabout services of Orpington Buses. RH11 is in High Street, Orpington, in 1987. *Keith Grimes*

Miscellaneous small buses

FS

The use of Ford Transits on urban bus routes in the early 1970s was unusual. It was only when local bus services outside London were deregulated in 1986 that there was an explosion in the use of small buses. Ford Transits normally had a six-year life in London. With a typical unladen weight of around 2250kg they were London Transport's lightest buses.

FS1-20	MLK 701-720L	Ford Transit	Strachans Pacemaker B16F	1972-73
FS21	GHM 721N	Ford Transit	Dormobile B16F	1975
FS22-26	CYT 22-26V	Ford Transit	Dormobile B16F	1979
FS27-28	C502-503 HOE	Ford Transit	Carlyle B20F	1985
FS29	C501 HOE	Ford Transit	Carlyle B20F	1985

● The bodies on FS27-29 were built by Carlyle on Dormobile frames.

Typical of LT's Ford Transits is FS20, the last of the original batch of Strachans-bodied buses delivered in 1972-73. This is a 1979 view shortly before the bus was withdrawn. When new the white relief band was carried over the top of the front wings and the bonnet.

The first five MAN-VW-based Optare CityPacers were in the maroon and grey livery adopted by London Buses' new Orpington Buses subsidiary. OV5 in Orpington shows the distinctive style of the first all-new product from Optare which had taken over the former Roe factory in Leeds in 1985. *Keith Grimes*

A leaflet to promote the central London Carelink service featured an illustration of one of the three Carelink-liveried Optare CityPacers, OV50-52. The circular route ran hourly and took almost two hours to make a round trip which connected Waterloo, Victoria, Paddington, Euston, St Pancras, King's Cross and Liverpool Street stations.

Carelink takes care of your London connections

OV

Optare was formed in 1985 to take over the former Roe factory in Leeds which was being closed by its owner, Leyland Bus. The 6.8m-long CityPacer was the first in a range of attractively-styled urban buses, and was the first Optare model supplied to London Buses. It was built on a modified MAN-VW LT55 light-truck chassis with a raised driving position to make it better suited for bus operation. The power unit was a six-cylinder turbocharged engine driving through an Allison AT545 automatic gearbox or, on OV1-5, a five-speed manual. The CityPacers typically operated for six years in London.

OV1	C525 DYM	MAN-VW LT55	Optare CityPacer B25F	1986
OV2-4	C526-528 DYT	MAN-VW LT55	Optare CityPacer B25F	1986
OV5	D529 FYL	MAN-VW LT55	Optare CityPacer B25F	1986
OV6-49	D338-381 JUM	MAN-VW LT55	Optare CityPacer B25F	1986-87
OV50-51	E998-999 TWU	MAN-VW LT55	Optare CityPacer B14FL	1988
OV52	E638 TWW	MAN-VW LT55	Optare CityPacer B14FL	1988

- OV1-5 were new to Orpington Buses in maroon and grey Roundabout livery.
- OV6-24 were for the C1, Westminster to Kensington, the first high-frequency midibus route in central London.
- OV25-49 were originally operated by London Country North West on LRT service C2, Regent Street to Parliament Hill Fields, in red livery. While with LCNW they were numbered MBV27-51
- OV50-52 were in a red and yellow livery for the Carelink inter-station service in central London.

SC/SD

Freight Rover was set up by British Leyland in 1981 in the hope that the prestige of the associated Land Rover name would boost sales of BL's light commercial vehicle models, which had previously carried Leyland or Austin Morris badges. The Sherpa had been introduced by Leyland in 1974 and was a competitor for the Ford Transit, although nowhere near as popular.

Two with Carlyle bodies were delivered new to London Buses in 1987 in a blue livery for the Chelsea Harbour Hoppa, a service part-funded by the developers of Chelsea Harbour. They were followed in 1990 by two second-hand Dormobile-bodied buses which were supplied by Carlyle in its capacity as a dealer. They were operated by London Forest on a contract for the Department of Health & Social Security and were returned to Carlyle in 1991 and replaced on the contract by two Metroriders.

| SC1 | D585 OOV | Freight Rover Sherpa | Carlyle B18F | 1987 |
| SC2 | D974 PJW | Freight Rover Sherpa | Carlyle B18F | 1987 |

- The bodies on SC1,2 were built on Dormobile frames. They were registered in Birmingham by Carlyle.

| SD1 | D811 KWT | Freight Rover Sherpa | Dormobile B16F | 1987 |
| SD2 | D212 GLJ | Freight Rover Sherpa | Dormobile B16F | 1987 |

- SD1 acquired 1990. It had been new to West Riding of Wakefield.
- SD2 acquired 1990. It had been new to Shamrock & Rambler of Bournemouth.

CV

The Omni was built in Shildon, County Durham, by City Vehicle Engineering and was based on a 1975 design by Austrian manufacturer Steyr. Unlike most other contemporary minibuses it was a purpose-built bus and it had front-wheel drive and 16-inch wheels which allowed for a low floor. The original Steyr design had a distinctive half-width driver's cab but CVE opted for a conventional full-width front with a large flat windscreen. The Omni was 6.65m long and was powered by a turbocharged four-cylinder Land Rover engine. Production by CVE started in 1988 and ended in 1990 when the company went into receivership. Limited production was started under new owners for a short time in the early 1990s.

| CV1-4 | F265-268 WDC | CVE Omni | CVE B20FL | 1989 |
| CV5-7 | A2-4 LBR | CVE Omni | CVE B23FL | 1989 |

- CV1-4 were registered in Middlesbrough by CVE.
- CV1-3 were operated by Westlink on behalf of the London Borough of Hounslow.
- CV4 was in red and yellow Mobility Bus livery.
- CV5-7 were ex C&M of Liverpool in 1992 as G195-197 CHN, and were operated by Westlink on behalf of the London Borough of Richmond which re-registered them as shown.

Typical specifications

Model	Engine	Displacement	Power output
Ford Transit	Ford	2.4 litres	62bhp
MAN-VW LT55	VW	2.4 litres	102bhp
Freight Rover Sherpa	Land Rover	2.5 litres	70bhp
CVE Omni	Land Rover	2.5 litres	85bhp

With front-wheel drive the Omni had a low floor, making CVE the unlikely supplier of the first London buses with step-free access. London Buses had seven, all of which were operated by Westlink. CV2 is in Ivybridge, Hounslow, soon after entering service. Noteworthy features are the prominent destination display, the single windscreen wiper and the external grab handles to aid boarding passengers. *Tony Wilson*

Miscellaneous coaches

Leyland

Between 1986 and 1992 London Buses purchased 23 Leyland coaches. There were 15 Tigers of which nine were bought new and six were second-hand. The air-suspended Tiger was originally powered by a horizontal 11.1-litre Leyland TL11H turbocharged engine and fitted with either Leyland's Hydracyclic transmission or a ZF manual gearbox, indicated by a Z suffix to the chassis code. Four of the Tigers delivered in 1990-91 had Cummins L10 engines, an option which had been introduced when it was becoming clear that there was no long-term future for Leyland's own engines.

There were also eight examples of the Tiger's predecessor, the Leopard. This had steel suspension, a Leyland 680 engine and Leyland's Pneumocyclic gearbox. These were all second-hand and were nine or ten years old when purchased by London Buses so were not in the first flush of youth. In contrast the second-hand Tigers were typically four or five years old so were still acceptable for front-line coaching duties.

LD1-2	C766-767 DYO	Leyland Tiger TRCTL11/3R	Duple Caribbean II C53F	1986
LD3	OMA 508V	Leyland Leopard PSU3E/4R	Duple Dominant II C49F	1979
LD4	OMA 504V	Leyland Leopard PSU3E/4R	Duple Dominant II C49F	1979
LD5	WGV 867X	Leyland Leopard PSU5D/4R	Duple Dominant III C50F	1982

- LD1, 2 purchased new by London Buses and originally in Tours and Charter livery.
- LD3,4 ex Crosville Wales, 1988.
- LD5 ex Beeston, Hadleigh, 1992.

LP1	GFV 183S	Leyland Leopard PSU3E/4R	Plaxton Supreme III C51F	1978
LP2	KAD 348V	Leyland Leopard PSU5C/4R	Plaxton Supreme IV C57F	1980
LP3	PWK 12W	Leyland Leopard PSU5D/5R	Plaxton Supreme IV C53F	1981
LP4 not used				
LP5-6	JVF 815-816V	Leyland Leopard PSU3E/4R	Plaxton Supreme IV C49F	1979

- LP1-3 were purchased from dealer Stanley Hughes in 1987.
- LP1 new to Robinson, Great Harwood.
- LP2 new to National Travel (South West).
- LP3 new to Smith, Alcester.
- LP5, 6 ex Cambus, 1989. They had been new to Eastern Counties.

TDL1	F789 GNA	Leyland Tiger TRCTL11/3ARZ	Duple 320 C53F	1989
TDL2	F791 GNA	Leyland Tiger TRCTL11/3ARZ	Duple 320 C53F	1989

- TDL1,2 ex Smiths-Shearings, Wigan, 1993.

TP1	A114 EPA	Leyland Tiger TRCTL11/2RH	Plaxton Paramount 3200 C53F	1984
TP2	A131 EPA	Leyland Tiger TRCTL11/2RH	Plaxton Paramount 3200 C53F	1984

- TP1 ex London Country South West, 1989.
- TP2 ex London Country North East, 1990.

London Buses bought nine new Leyland Tigers between 1986 and 1991. Leaside Buses TPL1 was new in 1989 and had a Leyland TL11H engine and a Plaxton Paramount 3200 body. It is in Alexandra Park in 1990. *Tony Wilson*

Metroline operated three Leyland Tigers which had been new to Smiths-Shearings, the Wigan-based operator of coach holidays. The first, in 1992, was TPL9 which had been new in 1987. It was a comparatively unusual version of the Tiger with a low driving position. It had a Plaxton Paramount 3200 body and retained the National Holidays livery it had worn with Shearings but with Metroline Travel fleetnames. *Tony Wilson*

MISCELLANEOUS COACHES

TPL1-2	G661-662 WMD	Leyland Tiger TRCTL11/3ARZ	Plaxton Paramount III 3200 C53F	1989
TPL3	G100 VMM	Leyland Tiger TRCL10/3ARZA	Plaxton Paramount III 3200 C57F	1990
TPL4	G608 SGU	Leyland Tiger TRCL10/3ARZA	Plaxton Paramount III 3200 C57F	1990
TPL5	G601 XMD	Leyland Tiger TRCL10/3ARZA	Plaxton Paramount III 3200 C55F	1990
TPL6	E771 WSB	Leyland Tiger TRCTL11/3R	Duple 340 C55F	1987
TPL7	H642 GRO	Leyland Tiger TRCL10/3ARZA	Plaxton Paramount III 3200 C53F	1991
TPL8	H643 GRO	Leyland Tiger TRCL10/3ARZA	Plaxton Paramount III 3500 C53F	1991
TPL9	D602 MVR	Leyland Tiger TRCTL11/3RZ	Plaxton Paramount III 3200 C53F	1987

- TPL1-5, 7, 8 were bought new.
- TPL3-5, 7, 8 had Cummins L10 engines.
- TPL6 ex West Coast, Campbeltown, 1991. It had a Duple body so should have classed TDL rather than TPL.
- TPL9 ex Smiths-Shearings, Wigan, 1992.

Other makes

	RUW 990E	Bedford VAL14	Plaxton Panorama C52F	1967

- This vehicle had been new to Homerton Coaches of London and was purchased from Sampsons of Cheshunt in 1975 to examine its twin-steering, a layout which LT was considering for its planned XRM double-decker (page 84). The VAL was not operated by LT.

AD/AP

These two vehicles were operated in London Coaches red livery. The 36ft-long 6U3ZR Reliance was powered by an AH760 12.4-litre engine.

AD1	AHE 996T	AEC Reliance 6U3ZR	Duple Dominant II C53F	1979
AP2	RPH 622R	AEC Reliance 6U3ZR	Plaxton Supreme III C53F	1977

- AD1 purchased from dealer Stanley Hughes in 1987. It had been new to Shaw, Barnsley.
- AP2 purchased from Hughes DAF in 1988. It had been new to Jenkins, Cranleigh.

BP

The YNT was an 11m chassis with a vertical Bedford 500 8.2-litre turbocharged engine mounted in mid wheelbase.

BP1	TRA 52X	Bedford YNT	Plaxton Supreme V C47F	1982

- On loan from Stanley Hughes group in July 1987. Received in white livery, allocated fleet number BP1, but not used and returned to Stanley Hughes.

Initial operators

Bexleybus	LD4	London Forest	TP1, TPL3, 5, 7, 8
East London Coaches	TPL6	London Northern	SKY1
Leaside Buses	TPL1, 2	London United	LP5, 6
London Buses	LD1, 2, TC1	Metroline Travel	LD5, TDL1, 2, TPL9
London Central	TP2	Selkent Travel	LD3, TPL4
London Coaches	AD1, AP2, LP1-3		

116 MISCELLANEOUS COACHES

Was this the most unusual vehicle to be owned by London Buses? London Northern SKY1 was a second-hand Neoplan Skyliner with 77 seats and a 16-litre Mercedes-Benz engine. *Tony Wilson*

SKY

The three-axle Neoplan Skyliner, made in Germany by Auwärter, was powered by a 352bhp 16-litre Mercedes-Benz V10 engine – the biggest engine ever in a London Buses vehicle.

SKY1	E469 YWJ	Neoplan Skyliner N122/3	Neoplan CH57/20CT	1988

- ex ILG, Leicester, 1991; operated by London Northern. It had been new to NAT, Leeds.

TC

The MB200 was DAF's mid-engined coach chassis, introduced to the UK in 1975. It had an 11.6-litre engine.

TC1	B593 XNO	DAF MB200DKFL	Berkhof Esprite C53F	1984

- TC1 was on lease from Ensign Bus, the Berkhof importer. It was in the livery of London Transport Tours and Charter (hence the TC classification). In 1987 it was renumbered DB1 in the London Coaches fleet.

DAF

Buses

When Dutch truck and bus builder DAF first tackled the British urban bus market in 1988 it did so in collaboration with Leeds-based coachbuilder Optare. The result was a stylish 11.8m-long single-decker on the new rear-engined SB220 chassis, with the complete vehicle being marketed as the Optare Delta. It was powered by DAF's 218bhp 11.6-litre horizontal engine and had a ZF automatic gearbox. The Deltas were the first full-size Optare-bodied vehicles for London Buses and were built using the Alusuisse system of aluminium extrusions.

London Buses operated 35 Optare Deltas, delivered between 1989 and 1993. They were based on DAF SB220 chassis. East London DA14 was new in 1992. The location is Cranbrook Road, Ilford, and the silver livery was inspired by an Optare demonstrator.

Initially the DAF SB220 was bodied solely by Optare, but Ikarus bodywork was made available from 1990. Ten Ikarus-bodied SB220s joined the London Coaches fleet in January 1992 for the 726 between Heathrow Airport and Dartford. They were shared between Wandsworth and Northfleet garages.

The Optare Spectra broke new ground in double-deck style, setting standards which other builders quickly followed. London Central SP15 is in Whitehall on its way from Oxford Circus to Crystal Palace on route 3. Although DAF provided the chassis, the vehicle was marketed as an Optare and has no DAF badging. *Tony Wilson*

Initially Optare had the exclusive rights to body the SB220, but from 1990 the chassis was also offered in the UK with steel-framed bodywork built in Hungary by Ikarus. London Buses' last new SB220s were ten with Ikarus bodies which were delivered in 1992 for operation by London Coaches on the southern orbital 726 Expresslink service between Dartford and Heathrow.

Following the success of the SB220 Delta, DAF's next cooperation with Optare was the DB250 double-decker, launched in 1991 as the Spectra. It was the first double-decker to feature Alusuisse construction and set new standards for double-deck bus design. London Buses ordered 25 which were delivered in 1992-93. The 10.1m-long Spectra had a 252bhp DAF RS200 8.65-litre engine.

DA1	F54 CWY	DAF SB220LC	Optare Delta DP49F	1989
DA2	F551 SHX	DAF SB220LC	Optare Delta B30+52D	1989
DA3-9	G931-937 MYG	DAF SB220LC	Optare Delta B49F	1990
DA10	G684 KNW	DAF SB220LC	Optare Delta B36+39D	1989
DA11-29	J711-729 CYG	DAF SB220LC	Optare Delta B40+31D	1992
DA30-35	K630-635 HWX	DAF SB220LC	Optare Delta B40+31D	1993

- All of the DA-class DAFs except DA2 were registered in Leeds by Optare.
- DA1 was new to Selkent and was re-registered WLT 400 before entering passenger service.
- DA2 was for Red Arrow operation. In 1990 it was rebuilt as B49F by Optare and then joined DA3-9 at Westlink.
- DA3-9 were new to Westlink for service 110, Twickenham to Cranford.
- DA10 ex Optare demonstrator, 1991. It was operated by East London.
- DA11-29 were new to East London in a silver and red livery inspired by ex-Optare demonstrator DA10.

| DK1-10 | J801-810 KHD | DAF SB220LC | Ikarus 480 DP44F | 1992 |

- DK1-10 were operated by London Coaches on the 726 Expresslink service. They were registered in Huddersfiield by supplier Hughes DAF.

SP1	K301 FYG	DAF DB250WB	Optare Spectra H44/27F	1992
SP2	K302 FYG	DAF DB250WB	Optare Spectra H44/23D	1992
SP3-17	K303-317 FYG	DAF DB250WB	Optare Spectra H44/27F	1992
SP18-20	18-20 CLT	DAF DB250WB	Optare Spectra H44/27F	1993
SP21-25	K321-325 FYG	DAF DB250WB	Optare Spectra H44/27F	1993

- All of the Spectras except dual-door SP2 were new to London Central for service 3, Oxford Circus to Crystal Palace.
- SP18-20 had registrations transferred from Routemasters RM1018-1020. The rest of the class were registered in Leeds by Optare.

Coaches

DAF introduced its mid-engined MB chassis to the UK in 1975. The first two for London, in 1984-85, had Berkhof bodies and came from Ensign Bus, the UK importer of the Dutch-built bodywork. DAF chassis became the preferred choice of London Buses when buying new coaches in the late 1980s, and these were supplied by DAF importer Stanley Hughes of Cleckheaton, West Yorkshire, which registered most of them in Huddersfield. The business was renamed Hughes DAF from 1988 after it was acquired by the Cowie group in 1987. Early purchases had Duple bodies built in Blackpool but from 1987 the standard body became the Van Hool Alizee, manufactured in Belgium. DD35/6 delivered in 1992 were Hughes DAF stock vehicles and were among the last Duple-bodied coaches to enter service. The Blackpool-based coachbuilder had closed in 1990.

The rear-engined SB chassis was offered in Britain from 1982 and initially used a vertical 8.25-litre engine where the MB had an 11.6-litre horizontal unit. London Buses bought SB chassis from 1986. These included eight SB3000s in 1989-90 which had vertical 11.6-litre engines. DV62, an SB2305, was the subject of a 260-mile *Commercial Motor* road test in 1991 where its fuel consumption was 10.4mpg.

The seven H-registered coaches delivered in 1991 had two breaks in the DV fleet number series because the DVLA retained the numbers 525 and 530 in the hope of selling them to BMW car owners.

DB1	B593 XNO	DAF MB200DKFL	Berkhof Esprite C53F	1984
DB2	C708 HWC	DAF MB200DKFL	Berkhof Esprite C49FT	1985

- DB1 was previously TC1 in the Tours and Charter fleet and was a former Ensign Bus demonstrator.
- DB2 was a former Ensign Bus demonstrator, acquired by London Northern in 1989.

DD1-3	D291-293 XCX	DAF MB230DKFL	Duple 340 C53F	1987
DD4 not used				
DD5	C645 LVH	DAF MB230DKVL	Duple 340 C52FT	1986
DD6 not used				
DD7-9	C27-29 MCX	DAF MB200DKVL	Duple Caribbean II C49FT	1986
DD42	E342 EVH	DAF MB230LB	Duple 340 C53F	1988
DD54	E654 KCX	DAF SB2305DHTD	Duple 320 C57F	1988
DD60	E660 KCX	DAF SB2305DHTD	Duple 320 C57F	1988
DD97	D297 XCX	DAF SB2300DHS	Duple 340 C57F	1987

- DD5 ex Welsh, Upton, 1987.
- DD7-9 were leased from Stanley Hughes for the London Liner express service to Birmingham.
- DD42, 54, 60, 97 on loan from Hughes DAF in 1988.

DD1-4	G901-904 MCX	DAF SB2305DHTD	Duple 320 C57F	1990
DD35-36	J35-36 GCX	DAF SB2305DHS	Duple 340 C57F	1992

- DD35-36 were operated by Selkent Travel and had the last new Duple bodies for London Buses.

DP1	B350 CJX	DAF MB200DKFL	Plaxton Paramount III 3500 C53F	1985

- DP1 was hired from Stanley Hughes for driver training in March 1986.

DP1	F637 OHD	DAF MB230LB	Plaxton Paramount III 3500 C53F	1988

- Acquired by Selkent Travel from Hughes DAF in 1992. It had been new to Stringfellow, Fleetwood.

DP60	D360 PJA	DAF MB230DKFL	Plaxton Paramount III 3500 C53F	1987
DP86	D286 XCX	DAF SB2305DHTD	Plaxton Paramount II 3500 C53F	1987

- DP60 on loan from Hughes DAF in 1988. It had been new to Smiths-Shearings of Wigan.
- DP86 on loan from Hughes DAF in 1991. It had been new to Smith, Alcester.

DV1	D133 ACX	DAF MB230DKFL	Van Hool Alizee H C51FT	1987
DV2-3	E312-313 EVH	DAF SB2305DHS	Van Hool Alizee H C51FT	1987
DV4	E604 LVH	DAF MB230LB	Van Hool Alizee SH C53FT	1988
DV5-6	E605-606 LVH	DAF SB2305DHS	Van Hool Alizee H C53F	1988
DV7	E607 LVH	DAF MB230LB	Van Hool Alizee SH C53FT	1988
DV8-11	F608-611 HGO	DAF SB2305DHS	Van Hool Alizee H C53F	1989
DV12	F612 HGO	DAF SB3000DKV	Van Hool Alizee SH C53F	1989
DV13-17	F613-617 HGO	DAF SB2305DHS	Van Hool Alizee H C53F	1989
DV18	F618 HGO	DAF MB230LT	Van Hool Alizee SH C53F	1989
DV19-20	F619-620 HGO	DAF MB230LB	Van Hool Alizee SH C53F	1989
DV21-22	F621-622 HGO	DAF MB230LT	Van Hool Alizee SH C53F	1989
DV23-24	H523-524 YCX	DAF SB2305DHS	Van Hool Alizee H C53F	1991

London Coaches' preferred vehicle was the DAF/Van Hool combination in a variety of specifications. DV11 was a rear-engined SB2305. It was new in 1989 and is seen here in Blackpool's Coliseum Coach Station soon after delivery. While all-over red appeared drab on buses it looked well on coaches. *Keith Grimes*

DV25 not used				
DV26-29	H526-529 YCX	DAF SB2305DHS	Van Hool Alizee H C53F	1991
DV30 not used				
DV31	H531 YCX	DAF SB2305DHS	Van Hool Alizee H C53F	1991
DV32-33	J432-433 NCP	DAF SB2305DHS	Van Hool Alizee H C53F	1992
DV34	J434 NCP	DAF SB2305DHS	Van Hool Alizee H C51FT	1992
DV35	J435 NCP	DAF SB2305DHS	Van Hool Alizee H C53F	1992
DV36-39	K536-539 RJX	DAF MB230LT	Van Hool Alizee C51FT	1993
DV51-52	F251-252 RJX	DAF MB230LT	Van Hool Alizee SH C53FT	1989
DV53-54	F253-254 RJX	DAF SB3000DKV	Van Hool Alizee H C53F	1989
DV55-58	F255-258 RJX	DAF SB2305DHS	Van Hool Alizee H C53F	1989
DV59-60	F259-260 RJX	DAF SB3000DKV	Van Hool Alizee H C53F	1989
DV61 not used				
DV62-63	G962-963 KJX	DAF SB2305DHS	Van Hool Alizee C57F	1990
DV64-66	G964-966 KJX	DAF SB3000DKV	Van Hool Alizee H C57F	1990
DV67	E648 KCX	DAF MB230LB	Van Hool Alizee SH C53FT	1988

- The Alizee H was 3.4m high; the SH was 3.55m high.
- DV32-35 were delivered to London Coaches in June 1992 after it was privatised.
- DV36-39 were new to Selkent Travel.
- DV67 was acquired by Selkent Travel in 1992. It has been new to Smith, Alcester.

DV19	D619 YCX	DAF SB2305DHS	Van Hool Alizee H C51FT	1987

- DV19 on loan from Hughes DAF in 1988. It had been new to Fishwick, Leyland.

Sample DAF specifications

Model	Engine	Displacement	Power output
SB220	DAF LC1160	11.6 litres	218bhp
DB250	DAF RS200	8.65 litres	252bhp
MB200	DAF DKFL	11.6 litres	260bhp
MB200	DAF DKVL	11.6 litres	280bhp
MB230	DAF DKFL	11.6 litres	260bhp
SB2300	DAF DHS	8.25 litres	244bhp
SB2305	DAF DHS	8.25 litres	265bhp
SB2305	DAF DHTD	8.25 litres	275bhp
SB3000	DAF DKV	11.6 litres	288bhp

Scania

Scania started selling bus and coach chassis in the UK in 1980. The chassis were built in Sweden. The company had previously collaborated with MCW in the production of integral single- and double-deck buses between 1969 and 1978, examples of which were bought by London Transport (see page 87).

The N-series chassis had a 257bhp Scania DS11 11-litre engine mounted vertically at the rear. The N113 was introduced in 1988, replacing the previous N112, and was suitable for both double- and single-deck bodywork. The SLW class were low-floor models which were accessible to passengers in wheelchairs. They had what was then known as kneeling suspension, in which air was exhausted from the front air bags to lower the entrance step at bus stops; commonplace now, but unusual in the early 1990s. They were broadly similar to the LLW class of Dennis Lances but were 11.5m long compared with 11.2m for the Lances and therefore had four more seats.

S1-9	F421-429 GWG	Scania N113DRB	Alexander R H47/33F	1989
S10-29	J810-829 HMC	Scania N113DRB	Alexander R H47/31F	1991
S30-31	J230-231 XKY	Scania N113DRB	Northern Counties Palatine H47/30F	1991
S32-45	J132-145 HMT	Scania N113DRB	Northern Counties Palatine H43/25D	1992
S46-71	K846-871 LMK	Scania N113DRB	Northern Counties Palatine H43/25D	1992

- S1-31 were Scania stock vehicles.
- S1-9, 30/1 were registered in Sheffield by supplying dealer Stuart Johnson of Worksop. They were operated by London Northern on the 263, Archway to Potters Bar.
- S10-29 were new to East London for services supporting the Docklands Light Railway.
- S32-71 were new to East London.

| SA1 | F113 OMJ | Scania N113CRB | Alexander PS B51F | 1989 |

- SA1 was a Scania demonstrator operated in 1989-90, initially by South London.

| SLW1-14 | RDZ 1701-1714 | Scania N113CRL | Wright Pathfinder 320 B37+33D | 1994 |
| SLW15-30 | RDZ 6115-6130 | Scania N113CRL | Wright Pathfinder 320 B37+33D | 1994 |

- SLW1-14 were new to Leaside Buses; SLW7, 10-14 entered service after the company had been privatised
- SLW15-30 were new to East London, and entered service after the company had been privatised.

In 1990 London Regional Transport introduced express bus services from Docklands to Waterloo and London Bridge stations to relieve pressure on the recently-opened Docklands Light Railway. From 1991 these were operated mainly by Alexander-bodied Scania N113s purchased from dealer stock. East London S16 is at Westferry, an area under development in this 1992 photograph. *Tony Wilson*

Volvo

Swedish bus and truck builder Volvo first appeared in the UK coach market in 1972 with the B58 chassis, and in the following year in the bus market with the Ailsa double-decker, developed by Ailsa Trucks, the company's UK importer. The Ailsa had a 6.7-litre turbocharged Volvo TD70 engine, mounted in the front overhang alongside the driver. It was not the most sophisticated of buses.

London Buses ordered three Ailsas as part of its Alternative Vehicle Evaluation programme, even though the chassis was about to be discontinued in favour of the mid-engined Citybus. So the Ailsas were a lost cause before they even turned a wheel in service. They had Alexander bodies, the first example of the Scottish builder's bodywork to be bought

The first Alexander bodies for London were three R-types on Ailsa chassis in 1984 which formed part of LT's Alternative Vehicle Evaluation. A1 is at Nine Elms. The concrete structure in the background is the Nine Elms Cold Store. *Tony Wilson*

On the last of the three Ailsas LT took advantage of the model's front-engined layout to locate the exit door in the rear overhang. V3 had two staircases, which reduced its seating capacity from 78 to 64. Note the unusual location of the rear number plate. *Tony Wilson*

by London. Two were conventional 78-seat dual-door buses but the third had an unusual layout, which featured an exit door in the rear overhang, along with a second rear-mounted staircase – much in the style of the New Routemaster three decades later. This reduced its seating capacity to 64 and also meant that in the interests of passenger safety it was crew-operated.

The three Ailsas were delivered in 1984. In 1987 they were joined by a dozen second-hand buses purchased from the South Yorkshire PTE and fitted with unusual Van Hool McArdle bodies manufactured in Ireland, and a further 50 Alexander-bodied buses which came from the West Midlands PTE. The second-hand Ailsas were operated for three years from Potters Bar and Harrow Weald garages, the latter in Harrow Buses colours.

The Citybus was developed from the best-selling B10M coach chassis and was powered by a horizontal 9.6-litre Volvo THD100 engine mounted in the wheelbase. This meant a high floor with a three-step entrance. London's first Citybus was delivered as C1 in 1985. This was an experimental vehicle fitted with hydraulic accumulators as part of Volvo's Cumulo

ABOVE: There's nothing about Volvo Citybus C1 to indicate that it features new technology in the form of hydraulic accumulators to capture energy from braking and thus reduce fuel costs. C1 was the first underfloor-engined double-decker in London and had an Alexander R-type body built to London specifications with a split-step entrance and opening front windows on the upper deck. *Tony Wilson*

BELOW: The bodies built in Ireland on Ailsa chassis by Van Hool McArdle were among the most distinctive on 1970s double-deckers. The big British customer was the South Yorkshire PTE, and in 1987 London Buses put a dozen 11-year-old ex-SYPTE buses into service at Potters Bar, where V6 is seen in the High Street. *Tony Wilson*

V62 was one of 50 ex-West Midlands Alexander-bodied Ailsas purchased by London Buses in 1987. Harrow Buses livery was applied to 29 of them.

system which captured energy from braking and was intended to save fuel; Volvo claimed it would reduce fuel consumption by up to 30 per cent. It was the first underfloor-engined double-decker to operate in London. The experiment was not a success. The bus operated from Palmers Green garage for around 12 months in 1986-87 and was then returned to Volvo where it was converted to standard Citybus specification before being sold to A1 Service in Scotland.

Standard Citybuses, the 39-strong VC class, were bought for London General between 1989 and 1991. The next new Volvos, also for London General, were 13 rear-engined single-deck B10Bs, powered by the same horizontal 9.6-litre engine as was fitted to the Citybuses. The Swedish-built B10B succeeded the Leyland Lynx, production of which had ceased in 1991 following the takeover in 1988 of Leyland Bus by Volvo. The B10Bs were London Buses' only single-deck Volvo buses. They operated in London for just four years, partly because their 11.8m length made them unwieldy.

An order for Volvo's Dart rival, the B6R, was placed for London General which was to take 21 with Plaxton Pointer bodies for service 295, Clapham Junction to Ladbroke Grove. Within weeks of the order being announced it was cancelled and changed to an extra 21 Dennis Darts when it became apparent that Volvo could not meet London General's delivery deadline. The Darts were delivered in 1992 as DRL53-73.

Seven second-hand Volvo coaches were acquired in the early 1990s, three of which came with the contract to provide transport for Digby Stuart College in Roehampton when it was taken over by London Coaches.

Specifications

Model	Engine	Displacement	Power output
Ailsa	Volvo TD70	6.7 litres	193bhp
B58	Volvo THD100	9.6 litres	230bhp
Citybus	Volvo THD101	9.6 litres	222bhp
B10B	Volvo THD103	9.6 litres	240bhp
B10M	Volvo THD100	9.6 litres	260bhp

VOLVO **127**

The only new double-deckers for London General while it was still part of London Buses were 39 Volvo Citybuses with 80-seat Northern Counties Palatine bodies. Brand new VC1 is posed on Westminster Bridge at the end of 1989, ready to enter service in January 1990 on the 133, Liverpool Street to Tooting Broadway via London Bridge, the route to which the first 27 Citybuses were allocated.

V1-2	A101-102 SUU	Ailsa Mark III	Alexander R H47/31D	1984
V3	A103 SUU	Ailsa Mark III	Alexander R H36/28D	1984
V4	LWB 389P	Ailsa B55	Van Hool H44/31D	1976
V5-6	LWB 408-409P	Ailsa B55	Van Hool McArdle H44/31D	1976
V7	LWB 375P	Ailsa B55	Van Hool McArdle H44/31D	1976
V8	LWB 394P	Ailsa B55	Van Hool McArdle H44/31D	1976
V9-10	NAK 412-413R	Ailsa B55	Van Hool McArdle H44/31D	1976
V11	NAK 416R	Ailsa B55	Van Hool McArdle H44/31D	1976
V12	NAK 420R	Ailsa B55	Van Hool McArdle H44/31D	1976
V13	LWB 369P	Ailsa B55	Van Hool McArdle H44/31D	1976
V14	LWB 377P	Ailsa B55	Van Hool McArdle H44/31D	1976
V15	LWB 387P	Ailsa B55	Van Hool McArdle H44/31D	1976

| V16-37 | JOV 766-787P | Ailsa B55 | Alexander AV H44/34F | 1976 |
| V38-65 | JOV 738-765P | Ailsa B55 | Alexander AV H44/34F | 1976 |

- V1-3 were part of the Alternative Vehicle Evaluation programme at Stockwell garage.
- V4-15 ex South Yorkshire PTE, 1987.
- V4 had the prototype of the new Van Hool McArdle body which was built in Belgium.
- LWB 387P was to have been V16. It was numbered V15 which had been intended for LWB 378P which was broken up for spares.
- V16-65 ex West Midlands PTE, 1987. Note how the 50 buses were grouped to match as best possible the fleet and registration numbers.

| C1 | C101 CUL | Volvo Citybus | Alexander R H45/33D | 1985 |

VC1-27	G101-127 NGN	Volvo Citybus	Northern Counties Palatine H45/35D	1989
VC28-38	G128-138 PGK	Volvo Citybus	Northern Counties Palatine H45/35D	1990
VC39	J139 DGF	Volvo Citybus	Northern Counties Palatine H45/35D	1991

VN1	K100 KLL	Volvo B10B	Northern Counties Paladin B40+23D	1993
VN2-6	K2-6 KLL	Volvo B10B	Northern Counties Paladin B40+23D	1993
VN7	K70 KLL	Volvo B10B	Northern Counties Paladin B40+23D	1993
VN8-13	K8-13 KLL	Volvo B10B	Northern Counties Paladin B40+23D	1993

DS1	RMU 967Y	Volvo B10M-61	Duple Laser C51F	1983
DS2	B127 PEL	Volvo B10M-61	Plaxton Paramount II 3200 C55F	1982
DS3	KJF 300V	Volvo B58-56	Duple Dominant II C53F	1980

- DS1-3 ex Digby Stuart College, SW15, 1990. DS3 was used solely as a driver training vehicle.

VP1	G91 RGG	Volvo B10M-60	Plaxton Paramount III 3500 C49FT	1990
VP2	F24 HGG	Volvo B10M-60	Plaxton Paramount III 3500 C53F	1989
VP3	H637 UWR	Volvo B10M-60	Plaxton Paramount III 3500 C50F	1991

- VP1,2 ex Park, Hamilton, 1993-94. VP1 operated by London Northern, VP2 by East London.
- VP3 ex Wallace Arnold, Leeds, 1994; operated by Metroline Travel.

| VT1 | YTA 612S | Volvo B58-61 | Duple Dominant II C53F | 1977 |

- VT1 ex Crawley Luxury, Horley, 1991; used as a training bus by Westlink. It had been new to Battersby-Silver Grey of Morecambe as CCW 936S.

London Buses' only Volvo B10Bs were 13 with Northern Counties Paladin bodies, operated by London General on the 88, Clapham Common to Oxford Circus, which was branded as the Clapham Omnibus. They had unusual personalised registration numbers: their KLL marks were the initials of London General managing director Keith L Ludeman. Similar bodies were fitted to the 31 LN-class Lances in the Metroline fleet. *Tony Wilson*

Dennis

With big-name international manufacturers like DAF, Scania and Volvo seeking to supply buses to London, the entry into service in November 1989 of a midibus from a small British manufacturer went almost unremarked. The manufacturer was Dennis of Guildford. The midibus was the Dart.

The Dart used a small Cummins engine, the 5.9-litre 130bhp 6BT. This was the turbocharged version of the 6B engine fitted to the MCW Metrorider, but mounted at the rear and driving through an Allison AT545 automatic gearbox. It provided more space, more comfort and a considerably improved environment for the driver in a vehicle which was little bigger than a Mercedes-Benz 811D. The MA-class Mercedes were 8.4m long and 2.2m wide;

There were 168 Darts with this style of body in the London Buses fleet. The early examples were built by Duple but most, including London United DT75, were built by Carlyle following Duple's closure.

By the time the DNL-class Dennis Darts were delivered to London Northern in 1994 London Buses' subsidiaries' new vehicles were appearing in a variety of brighter liveries. DNL110 is branded for the C2 Camden Link and is in Parliament Hill Fields in the summer of 1994. *Tony Wilson*

the prototype Dart was 8.5m long and 2.3m wide. The added sophistication of the Dart did bring with it a price penalty – when it was launched Dennis was quoting £51,000 for a complete Dart, which compared with around £40,000 for a Mercedes with Reeve Burgess body. The Dart had a GVW of 10 tonnes and ran on 19.5in wheels, where the Mercedes 811D had a 7.5 tonne GVW and 17.5in wheels.

In 1990 the Dart made a significant impact on London. An initial order was placed for 57, but this was soon increased, and very quickly orders had been placed for over 300 for delivery in 1990-91. The orders were quite a coup for Dennis. Most of London Buses' early Darts were 8.5m long, a size chosen so that they would be counted as midibuses when it came to drivers' pay rates. The DEL, DNL, DRL and DWL classes were 9m long. Few 8.5m Darts were bought by operators other than London Buses.

When it was first developed the Dart was to be bodied exclusively by Duple – both Dennis and Duple were then part of the Hestair group. However that changed with the closure of the Duple factory in early 1990. The production rights for the Duple Dartline body were acquired by Birmingham-based Carlyle which was the main supplier of bodies on London Darts in 1990. By the end of 1990 Wright of Ballymena was building bodies on Darts using the Alusuisse system of aluminium extrusions. Wright was joined in early 1991 by Reeve Burgess of Pilsley, near Chesterfield, with its Pointer. The Reeve Burgess factory closed in the summer of 1991 and production of the Pointer was transferred to the Scarborough factory of Reeve Burgess' parent company, Plaxton. The competition from Plaxton and Wright was too much for Carlyle which called in the receivers in the autumn of 1991.

In a quirky naming exercise Wright-bodied Darts DW1-14, based at CentreWest's Alperton garage, were given the names of constellations. These were, in fleet number order, Andromeda, Leo, Pegasus, Endamus, Rigel, Taurus, Orion, Nebula, Grus, Aquila, Regulus, Aries, Gemini and Equuleus. And if you take the initial letter of each name the list spells out Alperton Garage. Clever stuff.

By 1994 there were 718 Darts in London service with bodywork by Plaxton/Reeve Burgess (324), Wright (196), Duple/Carlyle (168), Northern Counties of Wigan (19) and East Lancs of Blackburn (11).

| DEL1-11 | L901-911 JRN | Dennis Dart | East Lancs EL2000 B34F | 1994 |

- DEL1-11 were new to London Central. They were registered in Preston by East Lancs.

| DNL101-110 | L101-110 HHV | Dennis Dart | Northern Counties Paladin B34F | 1994 |

DNL111 not used because the registration number 111 was retained for sale by the DVLA.

| DNL112-120 | L112-120 HHV | Dennis Dart | Northern Counties Paladin B34F | 1994 |

- The DNLs were new to London Northern, primarily for the C2 Camden Link.

DR1-10	H101-110 THE	Dennis Dart	Reeve Burgess Pointer B28F	1991
DR11	H611 TKU	Dennis Dart	Reeve Burgess Pointer B28F	1991
DR12-20	H112-120 THE	Dennis Dart	Reeve Burgess Pointer B28F	1991
DR21	H621 TKU	Dennis Dart	Reeve Burgess Pointer B28F	1991
DR22-31	H122-131 THE	Dennis Dart	Reeve Burgess Pointer B28F	1991
DR32-34	H532-534 XGK	Dennis Dart	Reeve Burgess Pointer B28F	1991
DR35	H835 XGK	Dennis Dart	Reeve Burgess Pointer B28F	1991
DR36-52	H536-552 XGK	Dennis Dart	Reeve Burgess Pointer B28F	1991
DR53-55	J653-655 XHL	Dennis Dart	Reeve Burgess Pointer B28F	1991
DR56-61	J156-161 GAT	Dennis Dart	Plaxton Pointer B24F	1991
DR62-80	J362-380 GKH	Dennis Dart	Plaxton Pointer B24F	1992
DR81-98	J381-398 GKH	Dennis Dart	Plaxton Pointer B28F	1992
DR99	J599 DUV	Dennis Dart	Plaxton Pointer B24F	1992
DR100	J610 DUV	Dennis Dart	Plaxton Pointer B24F	1992

The first Pointer bodies on Dennis Darts were built by Reeve Burgess, whose name is above the offside headlamp of London Central DRL1 on Peckham Hoppa service P11, Peckham to Waterloo. The Darts, introduced in 1991, had replaced Optare StarRiders. DRL1 was named Del Boy, the lead character in the 1980s BBC TV comedy *Only Fools and Horses*, which was set in Peckham. *Tony Wilson*

DR101-110	J101-110 DUV	Dennis Dart	Plaxton Pointer B24F	1992
DR111	J611 DUV	Dennis Dart	Plaxton Pointer B24F	1992
DR112-141	J112-141 DUV	Dennis Dart	Plaxton Pointer B24F	1992
DR142-148	K242-248 PAG	Dennis Dart	Plaxton Pointer B28F	1992
DR149-153	K149-153 LGO	Dennis Dart	Plaxton Pointer B28F	1992

- DR1-31, 53-55 were registered in Sheffield by Reeve Burgess.
- DR56-98, 142-148 were registered in Beverley by Plaxton.

DRL1-16	J601-616 XHL	Dennis Dart	Reeve Burgess Pointer B34F	1991
DRL17-28	K817-828 NKH	Dennis Dart	Plaxton Pointer B34F	1992
DRL29-37	K429-437 OKH	Dennis Dart	Plaxton Pointer B34F	1992
DRL38-52	K538-552 ORH	Dennis Dart	Plaxton Pointer B34F	1992
DRL53-73	K853-873 LGN	Dennis Dart	Plaxton Pointer B34F	1992
DRL74-95	K574-595 MGT	Dennis Dart	Plaxton Pointer B32F	1993
DRL96-98	K96-98 SAG	Dennis Dart	Plaxton Pointer B28F	1993
DRL99	K199 SAG	Dennis Dart	Plaxton Pointer B28F	1993
DRL100	K210 SAG	Dennis Dart	Plaxton Pointer B28F	1993
DRL101-108	K101-108 SAG	Dennis Dart	Plaxton Pointer B28F	1993
DRL109-110	K109-110 SRH	Dennis Dart	Plaxton Pointer B34F	1993
DRL111	K211 SRH	Dennis Dart	Plaxton Pointer B34F	1993
DRL112-135	K112-135 SRH	Dennis Dart	Plaxton Pointer B34F	1993
DRL136-146	L136-146 VRH	Dennis Dart	Plaxton Pointer B34F	1993
DRL147	L247 WAG	Dennis Dart	Plaxton Pointer B34F	1993
DRL148-158	L148-158 WAG	Dennis Dart	Plaxton Pointer B34F	1993
DRL159-164	L159-164 XRH	Dennis Dart	Plaxton Pointer B28F	1994
DRL165-169	L165-169 YAT	Dennis Dart	Plaxton Pointer B28F	1994
DRL170-171	L170-171 CKH	Dennis Dart	Plaxton Pointer B28F	1994

- DRL1-16 were registered in Sheffield by Reeve Burgess.
- DRL17-52, 96-171 were registered in Beverley by Plaxton.
- DRL53-73 were ordered in place of 21 Volvo B6Rs.

DT1-27	G501-527 VYE	Dennis Dart	Duple Dartline B28F	1990
DT28-57	G28-57 TGW	Dennis Dart	Carlyle C25 B28F	1990
DT58-70	H458-470 UGO	Dennis Dart	Carlyle C25 B28F	1990
DT71-74	H71-74 MOB	Dennis Dart	Carlyle C25 B28F	1990
DT75	H575 MOC	Dennis Dart	Carlyle C25 B28F	1990
DT76	H76 MOB	Dennis Dart	Carlyle C25 B28F	1990
DT77	H577 MOC	Dennis Dart	Carlyle C25 B28F	1990
DT78-79	H78-79 MOB	Dennis Dart	Carlyle C25 B28F	1990
DT80	H880 LOX	Dennis Dart	Carlyle C25 B28F	1990
DT81-87	H81-87 MOB	Dennis Dart	Carlyle C25 B28F	1990
DT88	H588 MOC	Dennis Dart	Carlyle C25 B28F	1990
DT89	H89 MOB	Dennis Dart	Carlyle C25 B28F	1990
DT90	H890 LOX	Dennis Dart	Carlyle C25 B28F	1990
DT91-98	H91-98 MOB	Dennis Dart	Carlyle C25 B28F	1990
DT99	H899 LOX	Dennis Dart	Carlyle C25 B28F	1990
DT100	H620 MOM	Dennis Dart	Carlyle C25 B28F	1990
DT101-110	H101-110 MOB	Dennis Dart	Carlyle C25 B28F	1990
DT111	H611 MOM	Dennis Dart	Carlyle C25 B28F	1990
DT112-120	H112-120 MOB	Dennis Dart	Carlyle C25 B28F	1990
DT121	H621 MOM	Dennis Dart	Carlyle C25 B28F	1990
DT122-156	H122-156 MOB	Dennis Dart	Carlyle C25 B28F	1990

The early Wright Handybus bodies for London Buses on Dennis Darts were plain, giving no hint of the attractive styling to come, as illustrated by the Pathfinder on page 136. CentreWest operated Wright-bodied Darts on its Gold Arrow services on which they replaced Alexander-bodied Mercedes-Benz 811Ds. DW42 of 1991 is in Carlton Vale on the 31 which operated from Camden Town to Chelsea via Kensington, a route which skirted central London. *Tony Wilson*

DT157	H157 NON	Dennis Dart	Carlyle C25 B28F	1991
DT158	H158 MOB	Dennis Dart	Carlyle C25 B28F	1991
DT159-163	H159-163 NON	Dennis Dart	Carlyle C25 B28F	1991
DT164	H264 NON	Dennis Dart	Carlyle C25 B28F	1991
DT165-167	H165-167 NON	Dennis Dart	Carlyle C25 B28F	1991
DT168	G349 GCK	Dennis Dart	Duple Dartline B28F	1989

- DT168 ex Duple demonstrator, previously numbered DD1.
- DT71-167 were registered in Birmingham by Carlyle.

DW1-66	JDZ 2301-2366	Dennis Dart	Wright Handybus B26F	1990-91
DW67-70	H367-370 XGC	Dennis Dart	Wright Handybus B26F	1991
DW71-99	JDZ 2371-2399	Dennis Dart	Wright Handybus B26F	1991
DW100	JDZ 2300	Dennis Dart	Wright Handybus B26F	1990
DW101-112	KDZ 5101-5112	Dennis Dart	Wright Handybus B26F	1991
DW113-126	LDZ 9113-9126	Dennis Dart	Wright Handybus B26F	1992
DW127-132	K127-132 LGO	Dennis Dart	Wright Handybus B28F	1992
DW133-168	NDZ 3133-3168	Dennis Dart	Wright Handybus B29F	1993
DW169-170	NDZ 3169-3170	Dennis Dart	Wright Handybus B26F	1993

- All registered in Ballymena by Wright apart from London General DW67-70, 127-132.
- DW100 ex Wright demonstrator, previously numbered DW00.

| DWL1-14 | JDZ 2401-2414 | Dennis Dart | Wright Handybus B35F | 1990 |
| DWL15-26 | NDZ 3015-3026 | Dennis Dart | Wright Handybus B35F | 1993 |

- DWL1-14 were new to Westlink.
- DWL15-26 were new to East London.
- DWL1-26 were registered in Ballymena by Wright.

Dennis Lance

Following the runaway success of the Dart, Dennis launched a full-size single-decker, the Lance, in 1991. This had an 8.3-litre turbocharged Cummins C-series engine and a ZF automatic gearbox and was a heavy-duty chassis running on full-size 22.5in wheels and with a design GVW of 17.6 tonnes. London Buses ordered 59 of the original Lance model with bodywork by Alexander (16 in 1992), Northern Counties (31 in 1993) and Plaxton (12 in 1994).

There was growing interest in the early 1990s in making buses more accessible to disabled travellers, and the first low-floor buses to enter service in London, in January 1994, were based on a revised version of the Lance. This was the SLF (Super Low Floor). It used the same drivetrain as the original Lance with a new chassis frame at the front which incorporated ZF independent front suspension. This eliminated the need for a step to clear the front axle. There were 38 Lance SLFs for London Buses and they were accompanied by 30 generally-similar Scanias. All 68 low-floor buses were bodied by Wright. The buses reportedly cost £8million which averaged out at around £117,500 per bus at a time when a conventional full-size single-decker cost just over £100,000.

LA1-10	J101-110 WSC	Dennis Lance	Alexander PS B39+32D	1992
LA11	J411 WSC	Dennis Lance	Alexander PS B39+32D	1992
LA12-16	J112-116 WSC	Dennis Lance	Alexander PS B39+32D	1992

- LA1-16 were new to Selkent. They were registered in Edinburgh by Alexander.

LLW1-24	ODZ 8901-8924	Dennis Lance SLF	Wright Pathfinder 320 B34D	1994
LLW25-29	L25-29 WLH	Dennis Lance SLF	Wright Pathfinder 320 B34D	1994
LLW30	L21 WLH	Dennis Lance SLF	Wright Pathfinder 320 B34D	1994
LLW31-32	L31-32 WLH	Dennis Lance SLF	Wright Pathfinder 320 B34D	1994
LLW33	L39 WLH	Dennis Lance SLF	Wright Pathfinder 320 B34D	1994
LLW34-38	L34-38 WLH	Dennis Lance SLF	Wright Pathfinder 320 B34D	1994

- LLW1-10 were new to London United.
- LLW11-24 were new to CentreWest.
- LLW25-38 were new to Metroline.
- LLW1-24 were registered in Ballymena by Wright.

LN1-31	K301-331 YJA	Dennis Lance	Northern Counties Paladin B37+30D	1993

- LN1-31 were new to Metroline. They were registered in Manchester by Northern Counties.

LV1-12	L201-212 YAG	Dennis Lance	Plaxton Verde B42+25D	1994

- LV1-12 were new to Selkent. They were registered in Beverley by Plaxton.

Specifications

Model	Engine	Displacement	Power output	Gearbox
Dominator (H2, 3)	Gardner 6LXB	10.45 litres	170bhp	Voith automatic
Dominator (H1)	Gardner 6LXB	10.45 litres	170bhp	Maxwell automatic
Dart	Cummins 6BT	5.88 litres	130bhp	Allison AT545 automatic
Lance	Cummins 6CT	8.27 litres	211bhp	ZF 4HP500 automatic

London Buses bought 59 of the original high-frame Dennis Lance chassis. The first 16 were for Selkent and had Alexander PS-type bodies. The paint glistens on LA5 in the summer of 1992.

After buying 16 Alexander-bodied Lances in 1992, Selkent took 12 with Plaxton Verde bodies in 1994. As illustrated by LV7 they were bought for the 208, Orpington to Catford.

Metroline had London's biggest fleet of Lances, 31 with Northern Counties Paladin bodies entering service in 1993. They had short lives in London, being taken out of service in 1997. LN19 is in Station Road, Edgware, on 12-mile-long route 113 which ran to Edgware from Oxford Circus. *Tony Wilson*

London United's ten Dennis Lance SLFs were London's first full-size low-floor buses. They were used to replace Metrobuses on the 120, Hounslow Bus Station to Northolt Station. There were 38 Lances and 30 outwardly similar Scanias. All were bodied by Wright of Ballymena with attractive Pathfinder bodies. This is LLW1.

Dennis Dominator

Before the successful Dart, the main Dennis bus model was the double-deck Dominator, launched in 1977 with a Gardner engine and a Voith gearbox. Dennis hoped to win business from operators of Fleetlines, a model which Leyland had announced it was going to discontinue. In 1984 London took three Dominators as part of the Alternative Vehicle Evaluation programme at Stockwell garage. The class letter H indicated Hestair, Dennis's parent company.

| H1-3 | B101-103 WUW | Dennis Dominator | Northern Counties H43/27D | 1984 |

Three Dennis Dominators were bought by London Buses in 1984 as part of its Alternative Vehicle Evaluation which was weighing up choices for future bus purchases. Dennis would indeed figure strongly in London Buses' future vehicle buying – but not with Dominators. The body was by Northern Counties. H3 is at Roehampton on a chilly day in February 1985.
Tony Wilson

Leyland Titan PD3A

For those who think London Transport's last front-engined Titans were the RTL-class PD2s delivered in 1954, think again. LT turned to Leyland when it was looking for new railway breakdown tenders in the early 1960s, ordering Titan PD3As. The PD3A was designed for 30ft-long double-deck bus bodywork, so although they weren't buses, the breakdown tenders did use purpose-built bus chassis, hence their inclusion here. The PD3A/1 had Leyland's O.600 engine and four-speed synchromesh gearbox. They were bodied by Mann Egerton of Norwich, a company which had supplied 130 single-deck bus bodies to LT in 1948.

1273-1277LD	571-575 EYU	Leyland Titan PD3A/1	Mann Egerton breakdown tender	1963-64
1278-1280LD	ALM 841-843B	Leyland Titan PD3A/1	Mann Egerton breakdown tender	1964
1416LD	JLA 72D	Leyland Titan PD3A/1	Mann Egerton breakdown tender	1966

Unusual breakdown tenders in the LT fleet were nine Leyland Titan PD3As with Mann Egerton bodies. 1275LD was maintained at Stockwell Garage where it is seen in 1979 shortly before being withdrawn. *Michael Baker*

Demonstrators

Over the years a number of manufacturers have supplied demonstrators to London. Those which were in London livery are listed here.

| UMP 227 | AEC Regal IV | Park Royal B40F | 1949 |

- UMP 227 was a prototype Regal IV, built to the then maximum length of 27ft 6in. It was evaluated at St Albans in 1950.

| | Leyland Olympic HR40 | Metro-Cammell B40F | 1950 |

- Leyland painted a preproduction Olympic in Green Line colours. It did not operate in London.

Leyland Tiger Cub demonstrator PTE 592 had an attractive 45-seat Saunders-Roe body. Despite carrying the Green Line name in Reigate in the summer of 1953 it is on Country Area bus service 447 to Woldingham.

The first of two Leyland B15 demonstrators evaluated by London Transport was NHG 732P, here waiting at Victoria before returning north on service 24 to Hampstead Heath. London would be the only fleet buyer of the model, which was unveiled as the Titan in 1977. The side panel promotes "Tomorrows Standards today".

	PHW 918	Bristol LS5G	ECW B45F	1953

- PHW 918 was owned by Bristol Tramways. It had a 7-litre Gardner 5LW engine and a five-speed synchromesh gearbox. It operated in Green Line livery in 1953-54.

	PTE 592	Leyland Tiger Cub PSUC1/1	Saunders-Roe B44F	1953

- PTE 592 was a Leyland demonstrator. It had a 5.76-litre Leyland O.350 engine and four-speed Pneumocyclic semi-automatic gearbox. It operated in Green Line livery in 1953-54. It was then retained by Leyland for use by the Leyland Motors Sports and Athletic Club.

	NLP 635	AEC Monocoach	Park Royal B44F	1953

- NLP 635 was an AEC demonstrator which was first registered by LT. It had a 6.75-litre AEC AH410 engine and a four-speed preselector gearbox. It operated in green livery in 1953-54, most of the time with Green Line fleetnames. AEC sold it to the West Monmouthshire Omnibus Board in 1957.

(RX1)	8071 ML	AEC Renown 3B2RA	Park Royal H44/31F	1962

- The Renown was a low-frame chassis and 8071 ML was an AEC demonstrator in Country Area livery. It was operated from Northfleet garage on the 480 (Erith to Gravesend) for a few months in 1963 after which it was returned to AEC who sold it to Osborne of Tollesbury. It did not carry the notional RX1 fleet number.

	VWD 451H	Metro-Scania CR111MH	MCW B37+29D	1969

- VWD 451H was the first prototype of the joint project by MCW and Scania to build a city bus for the UK market. It was in overall red with London Transport fleetnames and was evaluated alongside AEC Merlins at Plumstead garage at the start of 1970.

	NHG 732P	Leyland B15.04	Park Royal H44/27D	1975
	BCK 706R	Leyland B15.05	Park Royal H44/27D	1977

- These two Leyland demonstrators were evaluated at Chalk Farm garage on route 24 (Pimlico to Hampstead Heath) in 1976 and 1978. BCK 706R would be purchased in 1987, becoming T1131.

	7517 UA	Daimler CVG6LX.30	Roe H39/32R	1959

- This bus was on loan from Dennis in 1977 and had been fitted with a Gardner 6LXB engine and Voith automatic gearbox to test the powertrain to be installed in the forthcoming Dominator chassis. It was repainted in London red before delivery to LT and operated on the 27, Richmond to Camden Town. It had been new to Leeds City Transport.

	TOJ 592S	MCW Metrobus	MCW H43/28D	1977

- This was an MCW demonstrator painted in LT livery. It was inspected at Chiswick Works in December 1977 but was not used in service. It was repainted in Strathclyde PTE colours in 1978 and then in MCW demonstration livery before being bought by Stevensons of Uttoxeter in 1989.

DEMONSTRATORS **141**

With hindsight the Dennis Domino can be seen as a precursor to the Dart, not that anyone realised it at the time. London Buses DMB1 was a Domino borrowed from the Greater Manchester PTE. The body was by Northern Counties. It is in Junction Road, Archway.

| DMB1 | C760 YBA | Dennis Domino | Northern Counties B25F | 1985 |

- DMB1 was on loan from the Greater Manchester PTE in early 1986. The air-suspended Domino was a scaled-down Dominator chassis powered by a 5.8-litre Perkins 6.354 engine driving through a Maxwell four-speed automatic gearbox. It was used on the C11, Archway to Brent Cross, operating alongside Bristol LHs.

| DD1 | G349 GCK | Dennis Dart | Duple Dartline B28F | 1989 |

- DD1 was a prototype Dennis Dart and operated from a number of garages in the winter of 1989-90. It was purchased by London Buses in 1990 and numbered DT168.

| ME1 | G395 OWB | Mercedes-Benz 811D | Europa B26F | 1989 |

- ME1 was a demonstrator for Europa of Doncaster.

| MW00 | IDZ 8561 | Mercedes-Benz 811D | Wright Nimbus B25F | 1990 |

- MW00 was a Wright demonstrator. It was operated in the winter of 1990-91 and was then returned to Wright who sold it to Stevensons of Uttoxeter.

| DW00 | JDZ 2300 | Dennis Dart | Wright Handybus B26F | 1990 |

- DW00 was a Wright demonstrator. It was purchased by London Buses in 1991 and numbered DW100.

| | J135 PVC | Leyland Olympian | Leyland H47/25D | 1991 |

- This was a Volvo-engined demonstrator which was exhibited in London Buses livery at the UITP exhibition in Stockholm and was used briefly by East London before being sold to Capital Citybus in November 1991.

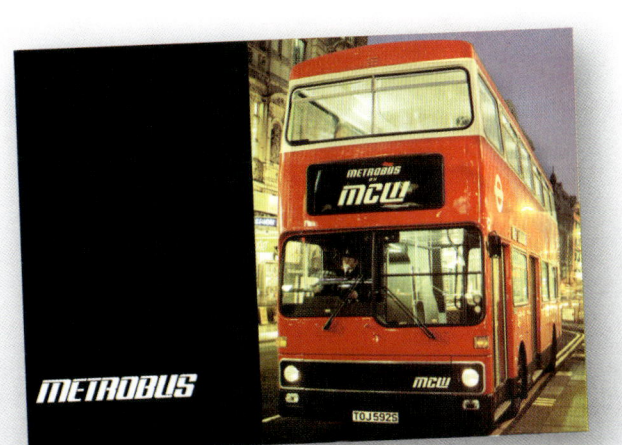

MCW's first Metrobus brochure featured London-liveried demonstrator TOJ 592S on the cover. It is posed in Piccadilly Circus, although the tight cropping of the image defeats the photographer's aim of showing MCW's new bus in the heart of London. This bus was not operated by LT. *Gavin Booth collection*

LT registration blocks 1939-1964

Before the introduction by the Department of Transport of year suffixes to vehicle registrations in 1963-64, London Transport generally booked blocks of registration numbers. During the war these blocks were small, but from 1947 to 1953, when there was massive investment in new buses, LT was reserving blocks of 500 numbers. Most of these were allocated to buses, and this list shows the allocation of registrations to both buses and support vehicles from 1939 to 1964. The list only includes those number series which featured buses. There were other, smaller, blocks of registrations which were used solely for support vehicles and there were also occasional one-offs, the most distinctive being PLE 1 on a stylish and luxurious 1954 Armstrong-Siddeley Sapphire used by LTE chairman Sir John Elliot.

Some service vehicles were initially operated on trade plates, often for prolonged periods, before a change of use saw them being registered. This explains why AEC 506 lorries which were built in 1928 appear on the list with 1939 FXT numbers.

Support vehicles were numbered in a straight series with a suffix letter indicating either the chassis make or the use to which the vehicle was put. Cars and motorcycles were not numbered. The suffix letters which appear in this list are:

A	Albion
AS	Austin
B	Bedford
C	Leyland Cub
CM	Commer
DG	Dodge
F	Fordson
J	AEC Regent
L	Leyland
M	Morris
P	AEC Matador
R	Road roller
X	Tractor
Z	AEC 506

The expensive luxury cars in the list, three Daimlers, eight Rovers and ten Humbers, were allocated when new to members of the London Transport Executive or to senior managers and where known their names are included. The lesser models from Austin, Ford and Vauxhall were used by departmental managers or as pool cars.

Much of the information on these pages has come from the London Transport Service Vehicles website (www.ltsv.com) which contains an amazing amount of data and is recommended to anyone with an interest in LT's support fleet.

Registration	Issued to	Date
FXT (400)		
FXT 41-48	TF81-88	1939
FXT 49-95	STL2601-2647	1939
FXT 96	Morris-Commercial Equiload van 416M	1939
FXT 97-98	AEC Regent breakdown tender 417-418J	1939
FXT 99	AEC Matador gully-emptier 411P	1939
FXT 100-103	AEC Matador tower wagon 412-415P	1939
FXT 104	Austin 14/6 saloon	1939
FXT 105-106	Austin 8 De-Luxe four-door saloon	1939
FXT 107	Morris Series II 10cwt van 419M	1939
FXT 108-155	CR2-49	1939-40
FXT 156-167	BSA 350cc motorcycle	1939
FXT 168-174	Austin 8 De-Luxe four-door saloon	1939
FXT 175-176	AJS 350cc motorcycle and sidecar	1939
FXT 177-326	RT2-151	1940-41
FXT 327	AEC 506 5-ton stores lorry 45Z	1928
FXT 328	AEC 506 breakdown lorry 52Z	1928
FXT 329-330	AEC Matador gully-emptier 409-410P	1939
FXT 331	Leyland Cub SKZ1 4-ton lorry 185C	1936
FXT 332	AEC 506 5-ton stores lorry 50Z	1928

Before booking blocks of 500 registrations (or 499 if the numbers started at 501), LT's biggest postwar block was 400 HLX numbers of which 388 were allocated to buses. These included 30 Country Area T-class AEC Regal IIIs with Mann Egerton bodies. T793 loads in Watford High Street.

FXT 333	Fordson 2½ ton tractor 349X	1931
FXT 334-363	Fordson V8 3-ton lorry 468-497F	1940-41
FXT 364	Commer 5½ ton lorry 499CM	1940
FXT 365	Fordson 1¾ ton tractor 467X	1940
FXT 366-367	Dodge 30cwt lorry 551DG, 565DG	1941
FXT 368	International Farmall tractor 600X	1941
FXT 369-370	Fordson 3-ton lorry 607F, 612F	1941
FXT 371-404	STL2648-2681	1941-42
FXT 405	STD101	1941
FXT 406-417	Fordson Thames 7V tipper 630-641F	1942
FXT 418	Albion KN127 lorry 125A	1937
FXT 419-427	B1-9	1942
FXT 428-437	STD102-111	1942
FXT 438-439	Fordson V8 fire engine 643-644F	1942
FXT 440	Lister auto-truck and trailer	1942

GLF (50)
GLF 651-700	G1-50	1942

GLL (50)
GLL 551-584	G51-84	1943
GLL 585-599	G86-100	1943
GLL 600	G85	1943

GLX (25)
GLX 900-924	D14-38	1944-45

GXE (50)
GXE 541-576	G101-136	1944
GXE 577	Albion KS127 tipper 365A	1939
GXE 578-590	D1-13	1944

GXV (25)
GXV 770-792	D39-61	1945
GXV 793-794	G137-138	1945

GYE (50)
GYE 51-62	D62-73	1945
GYE 63	Fordson Thames 7V tipper 649F	1944
GYE 64-82	D74-92	1945
GYE 83-97	G139-153	1945
GYE 98-100	D93-95	1945

GYL (200)
GYL 261-292	D96-127	1945
GYL 293-407	G154-268	1945
GYL 408	Fordson 1¾ ton tractor 465X	1940
GYL 409-460	G269-320	1945-46

HGC (200)
HGC 100-214	G321-435	1945-46
HGC 215-234	STL2682-2701	1946
HGC 235-254	B10-29	1946
HGC 255-299	D128-172	1945-46

HGF (200)

HGF 800-808	D173-181	1946
HGF 809-858	T719-768	1946
HGF 859-958	D182-281	1946
HGF 959-989	TD1-31	1946-47
HGF 990-999	STD112-121	1946

HLW (200)

HLW 51-105	STD122-176	1946
HLW 106-111	Bedford OLBD 5-ton lorry 655-660B	1946
HLW 112-115	Bedford OLBD 5-ton van 661-664B	1946
HLW 116-118	Bedford OLBD 5-ton lorry 665-667B	1946-47
HLW 119-130	Fordson E83W 10cwt van 668-679F	1946-48
HLW 131-138	Morris-Commercial PV van 680-687M	1946-47
HLW 139-250	RT152-263	1947

HLX (400)

HLX 81-438	RT264-621	1947-48
HLX 439-468	T769-798	1948
HLX 469-474	Bedford OLBC catering van 694-699B	1947
HLX 475-478	Bedford OLBC catering van 713-716B	1948

During the war small blocks of 25 or 50 numbers were the norm. The only numbers reserved in 1943 were 50 in the GLL series. G53 at Victoria is a Park Royal-bodied Guy Arab. *E G Masterman/The Bus Archive*

Most of the HLW block of numbers were used for buses, including 55 of the STD class Leyland Titan PD1s. STD171 passes Wellington Arch in 1953.

HLX 479	Austin 16 saloon	1947
HLX 480	Bedford-Scammell canteen 700B	1947

HYM (77)
HYM 765-841	trolleybuses 1765-1841	1948-49

JXC (500)
JXC 1-9	Bedford-Scammell canteen 701-709B	1947-49
JXC 10	Fordson E83W 10cwt police van 710B	1948
JXC 11-12	Austin K4LV 5-ton food van 711-712AS	1948-49
JXC 13	Fordson E83W 10cwt van 717F	1949
JXC 14	Fordson E83W 10cwt laundry van 759F	1949
JXC 15-19	RT652-656	1948
JXC 20	RTL 501	1948
JXC 21-164	RT658-801	1948
JXC 165-224	RT1402-1461	1948-49
JXC 225-324	TD32-131	1948
JXC 325	Fordson E83W mobile film unit 752F	1948
JXC 326-327	Bedford OSBT tipper 815-816B	1948
JXC 328	Bedford KD 30cwt lorry 860B	1948
JXC 329-331	Bedford OLBD 5-ton lorry 818-820B	1948

JXC 332	Fordson E83W 10cwt van 780F	1948
JXC 333	Bedford KZ 30cwt ticket van 838B	1948
JXC 334	Bedford OLBD 5-ton lorry 822B	1948
JXC 335	Fordson E83W 10cwt van 785F	1948
JXC 336	Ford Prefect saloon	1949
JXC 337	Fordson E83W 10cwt van 779F	1948
JXC 338-341	Bedford KD 30cwt lorry 893-896B	1948
JXC 342-343	Bedford OLBD 5-ton lorry 825B, 812B	1948
JXC 344	Bedford KD 30cwt lorry 865B	1948
JXC 345-346	Fordson E83W 10cwt van 774F, 768F	1948
JXC 347	Bedford KD 30cwt lorry 882B	1948
JXC 348	Fordson E83W 10cwt van 772F	1948
JXC 349-351	Bedford KD lorry 873B, 878B, 869B	1948
JXC 352-353	Fordson E83W 10cwt van 769F, 781F	1948
JXC 354	Mercury electric platform truck	1948
JXC 355	Ford Prefect saloon	1948
JXC 356-358	Fordson E83W laundry van 897-899F	1948
JXC 359	Austin saloon	1948
JXC 360	Austin 16 saloon	1948
JXC 361	Austin saloon	1948
JXC 362	Austin 16 saloon	1948
JXC 363	Austin saloon	1948
JXC 364	Vauxhall Wyvern saloon	1948
JXC 365	Austin 16 saloon	1948
JXC 366	Ford Prefect saloon	1948
JXC 367-368	Austin 16 saloon	1948
JXC 369	Vauxhall Velox saloon	1948
JXC 370-377	BSA motorcycle and sidecar	1948
JXC 378-392	BSA motorcycle	1948
JXC 393-409	Austin K4VT 5-ton lorry 900-916AS	1948-49
JXC 410-412	Bedford OSBT tipper 918-920B	1949-50
JXC 413	Fordson E83W 10cwt Utilecon 923F	1949
JXC 414	Vauxhall Wyvern saloon	1948
JXC 415	Vauxhall Velox saloon	1948
JXC 416	Austin saloon	1948
JXC 417	Bedford KD 30cwt lorry 858B	1948
JXC 418	Ford Prefect saloon	1948
JXC 419	Humber limousine	1948
JXC 420	Ford Prefect saloon	1948
JXC 421	Austin 16 saloon	1948
JXC 422	Austin K4LV 5-ton food van 922AS	1949
JXC 423-429	Ford Prefect saloon	1948-49
JXC 430-459	RT622-651	1948
JXC 460-489	RT1152-1181	1948-49
JXC 490-500	RT969-972	1948

● Humber JXC 419 was used by LTE chairman Lord Latham.

JXN (500)

JXN 1-179	RT973-1151	1948-49
JXN 180-312	RT802-934	1948
JXN 313-324	RTL1-12	1948

JXN 325-332	RT935-942	1948
JXN 333-342	RTL13-22	1948
JXN 343	RT943	1948
JXN 344	RTL23	1948
JXN 345-346	RT944-945	1948
JXN 347-439	RTL24-116	1948-49
JXN 440-443	Ford Prefect saloon	1949
JXN 444	Fordson E83W 10cwt van 773F	1949
JXN 445	Ford Prefect saloon	1949
JXN 446	Austin saloon	1946
JXN 447-448	Bedford KD 30cwt lorry 870B, 884B	1949
JXN 449	Fordson E83W 10cwt van 783F	1949
JXN 450	Austin saloon	1949
JXN 451	Fordson E83W 10cwt laundry van 755F	1949
JXN 452	Bedford OLBD 5-ton lorry 817B	1949
JXN 453	Bedford OSBT 5-ton tipper 917B	1949
JXN 454	Fordson E83W 10cwt laundry van 756F	1949
JXN 455	Bedford KD 30cwt lorry 886B	1949
JXN 456	Ford Prefect saloon	1949
JXN 457	Bedford KZ 30cwt van 840B	1949
JXN 458-459	Fordson E83W 10cwt van 784F, 791F	1949
JXN 460	Bedford OLBC 5-ton ticket van 809B	1949
JXN 461	Vauxhall saloon	1949
JXN 462-467	Ford Prefect saloon	1949
JXN 468	Bedford OLBC 5-ton ticket van 810B	1949
JXN 469-471	Ford Prefect saloon	1949
JXN 472	Fordson E83W 10cwt van 788F	1949
JXN 473-476	Ford Prefect saloon	1949
JXN 477	AEC Matador 7½ ton stores lorry 108P	1937
JXN 478	Fordson E83W breakdown van 924F	1949
JXN 479	Ford Prefect saloon	1949
JXN 480	Bedford KD 30cwt lorry 856B	1949
JXN 481	Vauxhall Wyvern saloon	1949
JXN 482	Fordson E83W 10cwt van 782F	1949
JXN 483	Fordson E83W 10cwt laundry van 757F	1949
JXN 484	Ford Prefect saloon	1949
JXN 485	Bedford KZ 30cwt van 842B	1949
JXN 486	Fordson E83W 10cwt laundry van 758F	1949
JXN 487	Bedford KZ 30cwt van 843B	1949
JXN 488	Bedford OLBD 5-ton lorry 814B	1949
JXN 489-490	Fordson E83W van 770F, 805F	1949
JXN 491-495	Fordson E83W 10cwt Utilecon 929-933F	1949
JXN 496	Fordson E83W 10cwt van 789F	1949
JXN 497-498	Fordson E83W 10cwt Utilecon 934-935F	1949
JXN 499	Bedford OLBD 5-ton lorry 827B	1949
JXN 500	Bedford KD 30cwt lorry 862B	1949

KGK (499)

KGK 501-650	RTW1-150	1949
KGK 651-720	RT1182-1251	1949
KGK 721-780	RT1462-1521	1949-50

KGK 781-916	RTL117-252	1949
KGK 917-928	RT946-957	1949
KGK 929-930	RTL253-254	1949
KGK 931-980	RT2122-2171	1949
KGK 981	G436	1949
KGK 982	Fordson E83W 10cwt Utilecon 936F	1949
KGK 983	Humber Pullman limousine	1949
KGK 984	Bedford OLBD towing lorry 826B	1949
KGK 985	Bedford KZ 30cwt recovery van 836B	1949
KGK 986-988	Bedford OLBD lorry 823B, 807-808B	1949
KGK 989-990	Fordson E83W 10cwt van 793F, 797F	1949
KGK 991	Ford Prefect saloon	1949
KGK 992-994	Fordson E83W 10cwt Utilecon 937-939F	1949
KGK 995-996	Fordson E83W 10cwt van 796F, 803F	1949
KGK 997	Vauxhall Wyvern saloon	1949
KGK 998	Fordson E83W 10cwt van 804F	1949
KGK 999	Bedford KZ 30cwt van 839B	1949

- Humber KGK 983 was used by LT deputy chairman John Cliff.

Registration numbers KGU 1-500 were all used for buses and were allocated to 259 RTLs and 241 RTs. RT2356 leaves Victoria Bus Station for Aldgate in 1970 on a short working of route 25 which ran to Becontree Heath. A cup of tea in the cafe on the right cost 7d (3p). *Iain MacGregor*

KGU (500)

KGU 1-100	RTL551-650	1949-50

KGU 101-200	RT2172-2271	1949
KGU 201-231	RTL255-285	1949
KGU 232-235	RT958-961	1949
KGU 236-243	RT1522-1529	1949
KGU 244-289	RTL286-331	1949
KGU 290-300	RT1530-1540	1949
KGU 301-400	RT2272-2371	1949
KGU 401-409	RTL332-340	1949
KGU 410-416	RT1541-1547	1949
KGU 417-439	RTL341-363	1949
KGU 440-450	RT1548-1558	1949
KGU 451-500	RTL364-413	1949

KLB (499)

KLB 501-600	RT1252-1351	1949-50
KLB 601-630	RTL414-443	1949
KLB 631-638	RT1559-1566	1949
KLB 639-654	RTL444-459	1949
KLB 655-678	RT1567-1590	1949
KLB 679-711	RTL460-492	1950
KLB 712	RT657	1950

LLU series numbers were used in 1950 for RTs, RTLs and 150 RTWs. RTW474 is in Camden town.

KLB 713-750	RT1591-1628	1950
KLB 751-850	RT2372-2471	1949-50
KLB 851	Bedford OLBD 5-ton lorry 813B	1949
KLB 852-853	Fordson E83W 10cwt van 800F, 766F	1949
KLB 854	Bedford KD 30cwt lorry 883B	1949
KLB 855-856	Fordson E83W 10cwt Utilecon 940-941F	1949
KLB 857-860	Ford Prefect saloon	1949
KLB 861	Vauxhall Wyvern saloon	1949
KLB 862	Bedford KZ 30cwt van 925B	1949
KLB 863	Fordson E83W 10cwt van 802F	1949
KLB 864	Fordson E83W 10cwt Utilecon 942F	1949
KLB 865-866	Austin FL1 hire car	1949
KLB 867	Bedford KZ breakdown van 926B	1949
KLB 868	Bedford OLBD 5-ton lorry 831B	1949
KLB 869-870	Fordson E83W laundry van 760-761F	1949
KLB 871	Fordson E83W Utilecon 943F	1949
KLB 872	Austin FL1 hire car	1949
KLB 873	Bedford KZ 30cwt van 841B	1949
KLB 874-875	Austin FL1 hire car	1950
KLB 876	Chaseside digger	1950
KLB 877	Vauxhall Wyvern saloon	1950
KLB 878	Fordson E83W 10cwt van 798F	1950
KLB 879-880	Vauxhall Wyvern saloon	1950
KLB 881-980	RTW151-250	1949-50
KLB 981-986	RT2116-2121	1949
KLB 987-988	Bedford KD 30cwt lorry 890B, 875B	1950
KLB 989-991	Bedford KZ van 887B, 834B, 844B	1950
KLB 992	Bedford KD 30cwt lorry 876B	1950
KLB 993	Vauxhall Wyvern saloon	1950
KLB 994	Fordson E83W 10cwt van 771F	1950
KLB 995	Bedford KD 30cwt lorry 871B	1950
KLB 996	Fordson E83W 10cwt laundry van 762F	1950
KLB 997-998	Bedford KD 30cwt lorry 879B, 855B	1950
KLB 999	Vauxhall Wyvern saloon	1950

KXW (500)

KXW 1-100	RTL651-750	1950
KXW 101-150	RT2472-2521	1950
KXW 151-250	RT3042-3141	1950
KXW 251-276	RT1629-1654	1950
KXW 277-284	RTL493-500	1950
KXW 285-300	RTL502-517	1950
KXW 301-343	RT1655-1697	1950
KXW 344-350	RTL518-524	1950
KXW 351-450	RTW251-350	1950
KXW 451-500	RT1352-1401	1950

KYY (499)

KYY 501-520	RLH1-20	1950
KYY 521-524	RTL525-528	1950
KYY 525-557	RT1698-1730	1950

KYY 558-568	RTL529-539	1950
KYY 569-632	RT1731-1794	1950
KYY 633-643	RTL540-550	1950
KYY 644-649	RTL1001-1006	1950
KYY 650-704	RT1795-1849	1950
KYY 705-715	RTL1007-1017	1950
KYY 716-720	RT1850-1854	1950
KYY 721-820	RTL751-850	1950
KYY 821-870	RT4218-4267	1950-51
KYY 871-970	RT3142-3241	1950
KYY 971	Vauxhall Wyvern saloon	1950
KYY 972	AEC Matador lorry 104P	1937
KYY 973	Bedford OLBD 5-ton lorry 824B	1949
KYY 974	Fordson E83W 10cwt van 777F	1950
KYY 975-977	Bedford KD lorry 864B, 854B, 861B	1950
KYY 978	Vauxhall Wyvern saloon	1950
KYY 979-985	Leyland Beaver tipper 944-950L	1950
KYY 986	Leyland Hippo tipper 951L	1950
KYY 987-988	Bedford KD 30cwt lorry 857B, 880B	1950
KYY 989-990	Vauxhall Wyvern saloon	1950
KYY 991	Humber Super Snipe saloon	1950
KYY 992-997	Bedford KD lorry 866B, 877B, 872B	1950
KYY 995-997	Bedford KD lorry 859B, 881B, 874B	1950
KYY 998	Bedford-Scammell low-loader 953B	1951
KYY 999	Bedford KD 30cwt lorry 885B	1951

- Humber KYY 991 was used by LTE member B H Harbour.

LLU (499)

LLU 501-600	RTW351-450	1950
LLU 601-640	RT3242-3281	1950
LLU 641-740	RT3842-3941	1950
LLU 741-771	RT1855-1885	1950
LLU 772-793	RTL1018-1039	1950
LLU 794-818	RT1886-1910	1950
LLU 819-830	RTL1040-1051	1950
LLU 831-840	RT1911-1920	1950
LLU 841-940	RTL851-950	1950
LLU 941-990	RTW451-500	1950
LLU 991-993	Bedford KD lorry 888B, 891B, 889B	1951
LLU 994-995	Fordson E83W 10cwt van 775F, 786F	1951
LLU 996-997	Fordson E83W 10cwt van 763-764F	1951
LLU 998	Bedford OLBD 5-ton lorry 654B	1946
LLU 999	Fordson E83W 10cwt van 776F	1951

LUC (500)

LUC 1-22	RT1921-1942	1950
LUC 23-28	RTL1052-1057	1950
LUC 29-40	RT1943-1954	1950
LUC 41-43	RTL1058-1060	1950
LUC 44-67	RT1955-1978	1950
LUC 68-79	RTL1061-1072	1950

LUC 80-100	RT1979-1999	1950
LUC 101-200	RT3942-4041	1950-51
LUC 201-225	RF1-25	1951
LUC 226-249	RT2000-2023	1950
LUC 250-265	RTL1073-1088	1950
LUC 266-281	RT2024-2039	1950
LUC 282-287	RTL1089-1094	1950
LUC 288-304	RT2040-2056	1950-51
LUC 305-319	RTL1095-1109	1951
LUC 320-325	RT2057-2062	1951
LUC 326-375	RTL951-1000	1950-51
LUC 376-390	RFW1-15	1951
LUC 391-490	RT4042-4141	1951
LUC 491	Ford Prefect saloon	1951
LUC 492-495	Fordson E83W van 795F, 801F, 799F, 794F	1951
LUC 496	Green 30cwt road-roller 962R	1951
LUC 497-500	Fordson E83W van 767F, 792F, 787F, 765F	1951

The MXX 1-500 block of registrations was used for both buses and ancillary vehicles. There were 479 buses of five different types, RT, RTL, RLH, GS and, as seen here, RF. RF462 looks unusually shabby for a London bus in this 1972 view at Hammersmith. *Iain MacGregor*

LYF (500)

LYF 1-33	RT2063-2095	1951
LYF 34-71	RTL1110-1147	1951
LYF 72-88	RT2096-2112	1951
LYF 89-167	RTL1148-1226	1951
LYF 168-170	RT2113-2115	1951
LYF 171-200	RT2522-2551	1951
LYF 201-276	RT4142-4217	1951
LYF 277-376	RT2552-2651	1951
LYF 377-476	RF26-125	1951-52
LYF 477-500	RT2830-2853	1952

LYH (50)

LYH 842-891	trolleybuses 1842-1891	1952

LYR (499)

LYR 501-635	RT3282-3416	1951-52
LYR 636-758	RT2652-2774	1951
LYR 759-825	RTL1227-1293	1951-52
LYR 826-827	RT2775-2776	1952
LYR 828-835	RTL1294-1301	1952
LYR 836-934	RT3417-3515	1952
LYR 935	RTL1307	1952
LYR 936-940	RTL1302-1306	1952
LYR 941-955	RT2777-2791	1952
LYR 956-961	RTL1308-1313	1952
LYR 962-999	RT2792-2829	1952

MLL (499)

MLL 501-512	RT2854-2865	1952
MLL 513-612	RF126-225	1952

Most of the NLE marks were issued to buses, including the last 167 RF-class AEC Regal IVs in 1953, all of which were allocated to the Country Area. This bus was one of a small number later rebuilt as Green Line coaches and here it is in Green Line livery, albeit operating on a bus service. *Geoffrey Morant*

MLL 613-675	RT2866-2928	1952
MLL 676-687	RTL1314-1325	1952
MLL 688-696	RT2929-2937	1952
MLL 697-703	RTL1326-1332	1952
MLL 704-712	RT2938-2946	1952
MLL 713-762	BEA coaches	1952-53
MLL 763-825	RF226-288	1952
MLL 826-925	RT3516-3615	1952
MLL 926-995	RF289-358	1952
MLL 996	Bedford OSBC 5-ton tipper 955B	1952
MLL 997	Humber Super Snipe saloon	1952
MLL 998	Bedford OSBC 5-ton tipper 954B	1952
MLL 999	Humber Super Snipe saloon	1952

- Humbers MLL 997/9 were used respectively by LTE member ABB Valentine and operating manager central road services J B Burnell.

MXX (500)

MXX 1-30	RF359-388	1952
MXX 31	RT2947	1952
MXX 32-35	RTL1333-1336	1952
MXX 36-39	RT2948-2951	1952
MXX 40	RT4668	1953
MXX 41-60	RT2952-2971	1952
MXX 61-130	RTL1338-1407	1952-53
MXX 131-208	RT3616-3693	1952-53
MXX 209-211	Bedford OLBC catering van 964-966B	1952
MXX 212	Fordson E83W 10cwt van 778F	1952
MXX 213	Bedford OSBC 5-ton tipper 959B	1952
MXX 214	Fordson E83W 10cwt van 1011F	1953
MXX 215-220	RTL1408-1413	1953
MXX 221-276	RLH21-76	1952
MXX 277-299	RF389-411	1952
MXX 300	Bedford OSBC 5-ton tipper 958B	1952
MXX 301-384	GS1-84	1953
MXX 385-386	Ford Thames E83W van 927-928F	1953
MXX 387-388	Ford Thames E83W van 974-975F	1953
MXX 389-490	RF412-513	1952-53
MXX 491	Humber Super Snipe saloon	1952
MXX 492	Bedford KD 30cwt lorry 867B	1952
MXX 493	Bedford KZ 30cwt van 835B	1952
MXX 494-496	Humber Super Snipe saloon	1952
MXX 497	Bedford OSBC 5-ton tipper 956B	1952
MXX 498	Humber Super Snipe saloon	1952
MXX 499	Ford Thames E83W 10cwt van 806F	1952
MXX 500	Bedford OSBC 5-ton tipper 957B	1952

- The five Humber Super Snipes were allocated to
    - MXX 491 chief engineer Percy Croom-Johnson
    - MXX 494 LTE deputy chairman A H Grainger
    - MXX 495 LTE member L C Hawkins
    - MXX 496 chief mechanical engineer road services A A M Durrant
    - MXX 498 chief supplies officer Eric Ottoway

NLE (499)

NLE 501-513	RTL1414-1426	1953
NLE 514-700	RF514-700	1953
NLE 701-739	RTL1427-1465	1953
NLE 740-750	RT2972-2982	1953
NLE 751-753	RTL1466-1468	1953
NLE 754-781	RT2983-3010	1953
NLE 782-786	Ford Prefect 100E saloon	1953
NLE 787-792	Ford Popular 103E saloon	1954
NLE 793-800	Ford Prefect 100E saloon	1954-55
NLE 801-900	RT3694-3793	1953
NLE 901-931	RT3011-3041	1953
NLE 932-999	RT4268-4335	1953

NLP (150)

NLP 501-561	RT4336-4396	1953
NLP 562-600	RT4569-4607	1953
NLP 601	Bedford OSBC 5-ton tipper 960B	1953
NLP 602	Bedford KD 30cwt lorry 868B	1953
NLP 603-607	Vauxhall Wyvern saloon	1953
NLP 608	Ford Thames E83W van 1021F	1955
NLP 609-610	Ford Consul EOTA saloon	1955
NLP 611	AEC Matador 7½ ton stores lorry	1936
NLP 612-614	Daimler Conquest saloon	1955
NLP 615-622	Austin LD01 1-ton van 1024-1031AS	1955-56
NLP 623-624	Ford Thames E83W van 1032-1033F	1955
NLP 625	Ford Thames E83W Utilecon 1034F	1955
NLP 626-627	Ford Consul EOTA saloon	1956
NLP 628	Leyland Beaver/Dyson low-loader 1010L	1953
NLP 629	Bedford CAV route survey van 989B	1953
NLP 630	Bedford OLDD 5-ton lorry 653B	1946
NLP 631-634	Ford Consul EOTA saloon	1956
NLP 635	AEC Monocoach demonstrator	1953
NLP 636-650	BEA AEC Regal IV coaches	1953

- The three Daimler Conquests were allocated to
    NLP 612 LTE member B H Harbour
    NLP 613 LTE deputy chairman A H Grainger
    NLP 614 LTE member L C Hawkins

NXP (249)

NXP 751-800	RT4397-4446	1953-54
NXP 801-848	RT3794-3841	1953
NXP 849-860	RT4557-4568	1953
NXP 861-920	RT4608-4667	1953-54
NXP 921-936	RT4669-4684	1954
NXP 937-954	RT4795-4812	1954
NXP 955-960	RTL1469-1474	1954
NXP 961-962	Bedford CAV ambulance 976-977B	1953
NXP 963-969	Rover 90 saloon	1955
NXP 970-999	RT4685-4714	1953-54

- The seven Rover 90s were allocated to
    - NXP 963 chief mechanical engineer railways
    - NXP 964 operating manager railways F G Maxwell
    - NXP 965 operating manager central road services J B Burnell
    - NXP 966 chief supplies officer Eric Ottoway
    - NCP 967 chief mechanical engineer road services A A M Durrant
    - NXP 968 chief civil engineer C E Dunton
    - NXP 969 operating manager country buses and coaches Geoffrey Fernyhough

OLD (363)

OLD 501-535	RT4715-4749	1954
OLD 536	RTL1601	1954
OLD 537-570	RT4750-4783	1954
OLD 571-576	RTL1475-1480	1954
OLD 577-589	RT4813-4825	1954
OLD 590-666	RTL1481-1557	1954
OLD 667-776	RT4447-4556	1954
OLD 777-812	RTL1558-1593	1954
OLD 813	RTL1337	1952
OLD 814-820	RTL1594-1600	1954
OLD 821-830	RT4784-4793	1954
OLD 831-860	RTL1602-1631	1954
OLD 861	RT4794	1954
OLD 862-863	allocated to RM1, RM2	-

SLT (100)

SLT 1-20	Ford Consul EOTA saloon	1956
SLT 21	Rover 90 saloon	1956
SLT 22-41	Ford Prefect 100E saloon	1956
SLT 42-48	Austin LDO1 1-ton van 1042-1048AS	1956
SLT 49	Coles mobile crane	1956
SLT 50-51	Bedford CA Utillabrake 1049-1050B	1956
SLT 52-55	BSA motorcycle	1956
SLT 56-59	RM1-4	1954-57
SLT 60-67	BSA motorcycle	1956
SLT 68-69	Austin LD towing lorry 990-991AS	1957
SLT 70-74	Ford Consul MkII 204E saloon	1957
SLT 75-77	Ford Anglia saloon	1957
SLT 78-100	Ford Consul MkII 204E saloon	1957

- Rover SLT 21 was allocated to LTE member A Bull.

VLT (296)

VLT 5-300	RM5-300	1959-60

WLT (699)

WLT 301-879	RM301-879	1960-61
WLT 880-903	RML880-903	1961-62
WLT 904-999	RM904-999	1961

ALH (100)

401-426 ALH	Ford Consul MkII 204E saloon	1960
427-441 ALH	Ford Prefect 107E saloon	1960
442-465 ALH	Ford Anglia 105E saloon	1960

466-480 ALH	Ford Escort 100E estate car	1960
481-493 ALH	Vauxhall Victor saloon	1960
494 ALH	Ford Thames 400E 12-seater 1152F	1960
495-497 ALH	RW1-3	1960
498-500 ALH	Ford Thames 100E van 1153-55F	1960
100 BXL	RM1000	1961

CLT (600)
1-253 CLT	RM1001-1253	1961-62
254 CLT	RMF1254	1962
255-452 CLT	RM1255-1452	1962-63
453-520 CLT	RMC1453-1520	1962
521-600 CLT	RM1521-1600	1963

DYE (265)
601-865 DYE	RM1601-1865	1963-64

The last big batch of numbers was the reversed CLT series allocated to 600 Routemasters, including 68 coaches with their distinctive twin headlights. RMC1464 leaves Guildford on the 60-mile run to Hertford. *Martin Llewllyn/Omnicolour*

Vehicle index

Code	Vehicle	Page
A	Dodge S56	106
AD	AEC Reliance	115
AP	AEC Reliance	115
B	Bristol K	26
BL	Bristol LH	78
BM	BMMO D9	81
BP	Bedford YNT	115
BS	Bristol LHS	78
C	Volvo Citybus	128
CRL	AEC Routemaster	57
CV	CVE Omni	112
D	Dennis 4-ton	81
D	Daimler CW-series	26
DA	DAF SB220	119
DB	DAF MB200	120
DD	Dennis Dart	141
DD	DAF MB/SB	120
DEL	Dennis Dart	131
DK	DAF SB220	119
DM	Daimler Fleetline	70
DMB	Dennis Domino	141
DMO	Daimler Fleetline	73
DMS	Daimler Fleetline	70
DNL	Dennis Dart	131
DP	DAF MB/SB	120
DR	AEC Regent V	81
DR	Dennis Dart	131
DRL	Dennis Dart	132
DRO	AEC Regent V	81
DS	Volvo B10M/B58	128
DT	Dennis Dart	132
DV	DAF MB/SB	120
DW	Dennis Dart	134
DWL	Dennis Dart	134
EC	AEC Reliance	62
ERM	AEC Routemaster	61
FM	Iveco Daily	108
FR	Iveco Daily	108
FRM	AEC Routemaster	58
FS	Ford Transit	110
G	Guy Arab	28
G	Guy Arab III	32
GLS	Leyland National Greenway	76
GS	Guy Special	33
H	Dennis Dominator	137
L	Leyland Olympian	98
LA	Dennis Lance	134
LC	Leyland Olympian	98
LD	Leyland Tiger/Leopard	113
LE	Leyland Titan PD2	82
LLW	Dennis Lance SLF	135
LM	Leyland Titan PD2	82
LN	Dennis Lance	135
LP	Leyland Leopard	113
LS	Leyland National	76
LSL	Leyland National	77
LV	Dennis Lance	135
LX	Leyland Lynx	100
M	MCW Metrobus	90
MA	Mercedes-Benz 811D	102
MB	AEC Merlin	66
MBA	AEC Merlin	66
MBS	AEC Merlin	66
MC	Mercedes-Benz 811D	103
MD	MCW Metropolitan	90
ME	Mercedes-Benz 811D	141
ML	MCW Metroliner	92
MR	MCW Metrorider	92
MRL	MCW Metrorider	92
MRL	Optare MetroRider	92
MS	Metro-Scania	90
MT	MCW Metrobus	90
MT	Mercedes-Benz 709D	103
MTL	Mercedes-Benz 811D	103
MW	Mercedes-Benz 811D	103
OM	BMMO D9	81
OV	MAN-VW LT55	111
RB	Renault S75	106
RC	AEC Reliance	62
RCL	AEC Routemaster	58
RF	AEC Regal IV	49
RFW	AEC Regal IV	51
RH	Iveco Daily	108
RLH	AEC Regent III	33
RM	AEC Routemaster	57
RMA	AEC Routemaster	60
RMC	AEC Routemaster	58
RMF	AEC Routemaster	58
RML	AEC Routemaster	58
RMT	AEC Routemaster	59
RN	Renault PR100	106
RT	AEC Regent RT	38
RTC	AEC Regent	42
RTL	Leyland Titan PD2	42
RTW	Leyland Titan PD2	45
RV	AEC Regent V	82
RW	AEC Reliance	62
RW	Renault S75	106
RX	AEC Renown	140
S	Scania N113	122
SA	Scania N113	122
SC	Freight Rover Sherpa	111
SD	Freight Rover Sherpa	111
SG	MCW Metrorider	93
SKY	Neoplan Skyliner N122	116
SLW	Scania N113	122
SM	AEC Swift	66
SMS	AEC Swift	66
SP	DAF DB250	119
SR	Mercedes-Benz 811D	104
SRM	AEC Routemaster	61
SRT	AEC Regent	47
ST	AEC Regent	81
STD	Leyland Titan PD1	32
STL	AEC Regent II	32
T	AEC Regal	32
T	Leyland Titan	96
TC	DAF MB200	116
TD	Leyland Tiger PS1	32
TDL	Leyland Tiger TRC	113
TP	Leyland Tiger TRC	113
TPL	Leyland Tiger TRC	115
TT	Thames 570E	80
V	Ailsa	127
VC	Volvo Citybus	128
VN	Volvo B10B	128
VP	Volvo B10M	128
VT	Volvo B58	128
XA	Leyland Atlantean	68
XF	Daimler Fleetline	68
XMB	AEC Merlin	66
XMS	AEC Merlin	66
XRM	Unrealised projects	84
	BEA coaches	52
	BUT trolleybuses	34
	Demonstrators	139
	Leyland Titan PD3A	138

TAILPIECE

This summer 1979 picture neatly sums up London's perceived problem with buses which it hadn't designed itself. On the left Fleetline DMS1372 stands at the roadside with its engine cover open, letting other road users know that it has broken down and is awaiting attention from LT's engineers. Although only seven years old the Fleetline would be sold for scrap later in 1979. On the right is a sign of the new order, MCW Metrobus M48 in the attractive but short-lived livery with white upper deck window surrounds.